BLACKSTONE GRIDDLE MADE EASY

No-Stress Blackstone Grilling | Quick, Tasty & Foolproof Recipes with Pro Techniques to Get It Right the First Time

Aiken Carter

© 2025 Blackstone Griddle Made Easy All rights reserved. This book, 'Blackstone Griddle Made Easy', is designed purely for educational purposes. The publisher accepts no liability for any harm or loss arising from the application or misapplication of the content herein. All trademarks and brand names referenced are owned by their respective companies. This book is provided "as is", without any guarantees, whether explicit or implicit. Any unauthorized copying, sharing, or dissemination of this book, in full or in part, is strictly forbidden.

Table of Contents

Chapter 1: Getting Started with Your Griddle 5

Understanding Your Blackstone Griddle 6

    Setting Up for the First Time 7

    Essential Grilling Tools 7

Basic Techniques and Tips 8

    Preheating and Temperature Control 9

    Cleaning and Maintenance 9

Chapter 2: 30 Breakfast Recipes 11

1. Pancake Stack with Maple Syrup 11
2. Breakfast Burrito with Sausage and Eggs 12
3. Griddled French Toast with Berries 12
4. Crispy Bacon and Egg Sandwich 13
5. Griddle-Cooked Hash Browns 14
6. Blueberry Pancakes with Lemon Zest 15
7. Grilled Banana and Nutella Wrap 16
8. Classic Eggs Benedict on the Griddle 17
9. Griddle-Seared Avocado Toast 18
10. Cheddar and Chive Omelette 18
11. Cinnamon Roll Pancakes 19
12. Smoked Salmon and Cream Cheese Bagel 20
13. Griddled Breakfast Quesadilla 21
14. Spinach and Feta Omelette 22
15. Griddled Corned Beef Hash 23
16. Apple Cinnamon Griddle Cakes 24
17. Grilled Breakfast Pizza 24
18. Sautéed Mushrooms and Spinach Frittata 25
19. Griddle-Cooked Breakfast Tacos 26
20. Sweet Potato and Black Bean Hash 27
21. Griddled Sourdough with Avocado and Poached Egg 28
22. Griddle-Cooked Chorizo and Egg Skillet 29
23. Grilled Veggie and Cheese Scramble 30
24. Buttermilk Pancakes with Fresh Fruit 31
25. Griddled Canadian Bacon and Egg Muffin 32
26. Grilled Breakfast Burrito Bowl 33
27. Griddle-Seared Turkey Sausage Patties 33
28. Griddled Peanut Butter and Banana Sandwich 34
29. Griddle-Cooked Oatmeal Pancakes 35
30. Grilled Zucchini and Egg Whites Omelette 36

Chapter 3: 30 Lunch Recipes 38

31. Griddled Chicken Caesar Wrap 38
32. Grilled Portobello Mushroom Burger 39
33. Griddle-Seared Steak Fajitas 39
34. Honey Mustard Chicken Skewers 40
35. Grilled Shrimp Tacos with Lime Slaw 41
36. Griddled Turkey and Avocado Panini 42
37. Blackstone Grilled Cheese with Tomato Soup 43
38. Griddle-Cooked Philly Cheesesteak 44
39. Grilled Veggie and Hummus Wrap 45
40. Griddle-Seared Tuna Melt 46
41. Griddled Chicken Quesadilla 47
42. Grilled Caprese Sandwich 47
43. Griddle-Cooked Reuben Sandwich 48
44. Griddled BBQ Pulled Pork Sliders 49
45. Grilled Mediterranean Chicken Salad 50
46. Griddle-Seared Beef and Broccoli Stir Fry 51
47. Griddled Teriyaki Chicken Bowl 52
48. Grilled Fish Tacos with Mango Salsa 52
49. Griddle-Cooked Buffalo Chicken Wrap 53
50. Grilled Italian Sausage and Peppers 54
51. Griddled Ham and Swiss on Rye 55
52. Griddle-Seared Veggie Burger 56
53. Grilled Margherita Flatbread 56
54. Griddled Chicken Pesto Panini 57
55. Grilled Cuban Sandwich 58
56. Griddle-Cooked Asian Lettuce Wraps 59
57. Griddled Lobster Roll 60

58. Grilled Chicken Gyros with Tzatziki 61
59. Griddle-Seared Eggplant Parmesan 61
60. Grilled Sweet Chili Tofu Sandwich 62

BONUS 64

Chapter 4: 30 Dinner Recipes 65

61. Griddled Lemon Herb Chicken 65
62. Grilled Garlic Butter Shrimp 65
63. Blackstone Griddle-Seared Lamb Chops 66
64. Grilled Balsamic Glazed Steak 67
65. Griddled Honey Garlic Salmon 68
66. Grilled Cajun Chicken Alfredo 68
67. Griddled BBQ Chicken Breasts 69
68. Grilled Chimichurri Flank Steak 70
69. Blackstone Griddle-Cooked Stuffed Bell Peppers 71
70. Griddled Lemon Dill Tilapia 72
71. Grilled Teriyaki Pork Chops 72
72. Griddled Mushroom and Swiss Burger 73
73. Grilled Thai Peanut Chicken Skewers 74
74. Griddle-Cooked Chicken Fajita Quesadillas 75
75. Grilled Pineapple Teriyaki Chicken 76
76. Griddled Rosemary Garlic Pork Tenderloin 77
77. Grilled Jerk Chicken with Pineapple Salsa 77
78. Blackstone Griddle-Seared Scallops with Garlic Butter 78
79. Griddled Sweet and Spicy BBQ Ribs 79
80. Grilled Honey Sriracha Chicken Thighs 80
81. Griddled Herb-Crusted Salmon Fillets 81
82. Grilled Mediterranean Lamb Kebabs 81
83. Griddled Blackened Catfish 82
84. Grilled Hoisin Glazed Pork Ribs 83
85. Griddled Italian Chicken Cutlets 84
86. Grilled Lemon Pepper Tilapia 85
87. Griddled Asian Style Pork Chops 85
88. Grilled Caribbean Jerk Shrimp 86
89. Griddled Maple Glazed Pork Belly 87
90. Grilled Chipotle Lime Chicken 88

Chapter 5: 30 Sides and Snacks Recipes 89

91. Griddled Garlic Parmesan Asparagus 89
92. Grilled Corn on the Cob with Lime Butter 89
93. Griddle-Cooked Zucchini Fritters 90
94. Grilled Halloumi with Cherry Tomatoes 91
95. Griddled Sweet Potato Wedges 91
96. Grilled Jalapeño Poppers with Cream Cheese 92
97. Griddle-Seared Brussels Sprouts with Bacon 93
98. Grilled Artichoke Hearts with Lemon Aioli 93
99. Griddled Cheesy Cauliflower Bites 94
100. Grilled Stuffed Mini Bell Peppers 95
101. Griddle-Cooked Spinach and Cheese Stuffed Mushrooms 95
102. Grilled Avocado with Lime and Chili 96
103. Griddled Rosemary Garlic Flatbread 97
104. Grilled Buffalo Cauliflower Bites 97
105. Griddle-Seared Polenta Cakes with Marinara 98
106. Grilled Peach and Burrata Salad 99
107. Griddled Eggplant Caponata 100
108. Grilled Pineapple Salsa 100
109. Griddle-Cooked Cheese-Stuffed Jalapeños 101
110. Grilled Garlic Herb Potato Skewers 102
111. Griddled Crispy Chickpeas with Smoked Paprika 102
112. Grilled Lemon Basil Shrimp Skewers 103
113. Griddle-Seared Sweet Corn Fritters 104
114. Grilled Balsamic Glazed Portobello Mushrooms 104
115. Griddled BBQ Cauliflower Bites 105
116. Grilled Watermelon and Feta Salad 105
117. Griddle-Cooked Spinach Artichoke Dip 106
118. Grilled Prosciutto-Wrapped Asparagus 107
119. Griddled Chimichurri Grilled Vegetables 108
120. Grilled Tomato and Mozzarella Skewers 108

Conclusion 110

Chapter 1: Getting Started with Your Griddle

Initiating your journey with Blackstone grilling requires a solid grasp of the essential components that make up your Blackstone Griddle. This flat-top cooking tool is crafted to provide a versatile culinary platform, capable of accommodating a wide variety of food items, from breakfast staples like pancakes and eggs to dinner favorites such as steaks and stir-fries. It's important to familiarize yourself with the griddle's structural design and its unique features. Typically, Blackstone Griddles are made from cold-rolled steel, a material celebrated for its durability and its ability to distribute heat evenly across the surface. Before its first use, seasoning your griddle becomes a vital step, as it creates a non-stick coating and protects the surface from oxidation and corrosion. This seasoning process involves applying a thin, even layer of oil over the griddle top and heating it until the oil reaches its smoking point. Repeating this process several times builds up a tough protective layer.

Mastering the preheating process of your Blackstone Griddle is another crucial skill. A properly preheated griddle guarantees that the cooking surface attains the ideal temperature, which is essential for achieving that perfect sear on your food. Start by preheating the griddle for about 10 to 15 minutes, adjusting to a temperature range suited to the specific food you're preparing. More delicate items, like eggs or pancakes, need a lower temperature to avoid burning, while searing meats requires a higher heat intensity.

Understanding the temperature zones that naturally form on your griddle surface can significantly boost your cooking abilities. The large surface area of the griddle naturally creates areas of varying heat levels, allowing you to cook multiple food items at once by using hotter zones for searing while reserving cooler areas for slower cooking or keeping items warm. Effectively managing these thermal zones enables you to prepare a complete meal, including proteins, vegetables, and other components, all on a single cooking surface.

Maintaining your Blackstone Griddle is crucial for ensuring its longevity and consistent performance. Regular cleaning after each use is important to avoid residue buildup and to preserve the seasoning layer. Once the griddle has cooled to a warm temperature, it's wise to use a metal scraper to remove any food remnants. Afterward, wipe down the surface with a cloth or paper towel dampened with water or a mild detergent to ensure it's clean. Applying a thin layer of cooking oil after cleaning is key to safeguarding the surface until its next use.

Equipping yourself with the right tools and accessories can significantly enhance the effectiveness and enjoyment of your Blackstone grilling experiences. Essential tools include a sturdy spatula for flipping and maneuvering food, and tongs, which are crucial for handling items like vegetables or meat. A basting cover is also handy for tasks such as melting cheese or steaming veggies. Additional accessories, like a breakfast kit designed for pancakes and eggs or a pizza kit meant for grilling pizzas, can introduce fresh and exciting ways to maximize the potential of the griddle.

To refine your skills with the Blackstone griddle, it's important to grasp the selection of the right oil for both cooking and seasoning processes. Oils are defined by their smoke points, which indicate the specific temperature at which they start to smoke and eventually break down. For seasoning the griddle, it's crucial to choose oils with high smoke points, such as canola oil, vegetable oil, or flaxseed oil. These oils are preferred because they can withstand higher temperatures without degrading, thus creating a strong, non-stick surface that boosts the griddle's durability and performance. When cooking, the oil selection should be carefully matched with the desired flavor profile and the specific temperature needs of the dish. Olive oil, with its distinctive taste, is particularly ideal for medium-heat cooking, adding a unique flavor to your food. On the other hand, grapeseed oil, recognized for its neutral flavor and high smoke point, is versatile enough to be effectively used across various temperatures, accommodating both high-heat searing and low-temperature cooking with ease.

Effectively managing the temperature on the Blackstone griddle requires a thoughtful and nuanced approach. While the initial preheating phase is vital to prepare the cooking surface, making real-time adjustments to the flame intensity during cooking is equally important to meet the specific requirements of each dish. For example, when flipping a steak to sear the other side, it can be advantageous to slightly lower the heat to prevent overcooking and ensure the meat stays juicy. Conversely, to achieve a delightfully crispy skin on fish or chicken, a temporary boost in heat can be used to enhance the texture without losing moisture. This dynamic temperature control technique is key to ensuring that every element of your meal is cooked to perfection, maintaining both flavor and texture.

A professional technique that can significantly enhance your cooking efficiency involves the strategic use of temperature zones on the griddle. By assigning specific areas of the griddle for different temperature ranges, you can cook various foods simultaneously at their ideal temperatures, optimizing the cooking sequence. Start by placing items that need higher temperatures and longer cooking times in the hotter zones. Once these items are properly cooked, they can be moved to a cooler part of the griddle to keep warm, allowing you to focus on preparing more delicate items in the hotter sections. This organized approach ensures that all components of your meal are served at their freshest and at the right temperature, exactly when they're meant to be enjoyed.

One of the most rewarding aspects of using the Blackstone griddle is the wide range of culinary creations it enables. The griddle's versatility allows you to prepare everything from perfectly grilled burgers and hot dogs to intricate hibachi-style dishes and gourmet pizzas. The secret to maximizing the potential of the Blackstone griddle lies in your willingness to experiment and try out new techniques or recipes without hesitation. The griddle's forgiving nature and adaptability make it an excellent platform for culinary innovation, encouraging cooks to stretch the limits of their creativity and craft an ever-evolving collection of delicious dishes.

Understanding Your Blackstone Griddle

Understanding the intricate details of temperature control and maintenance is just the first step when working with your Blackstone Griddle. A solid grasp of the fuel source and the ignition process is essential for optimal operation. Most Blackstone Griddles use propane gas as their main fuel source, which is popular for its ability to provide quick start-ups and maintain steady, even heat distribution across the cooking surface. To ensure both safety and efficiency, it's vital to regularly check for potential propane tank leaks. You can do this by applying a mixture of dish soap and water to the connection points where the propane tank meets the griddle. With the gas on, keep a close eye out for bubbles forming at these junctions. If you see bubbles, it indicates a leak, and you should take immediate action to either tighten the connections or replace any faulty components before trying to ignite the griddle.

To start the ignition process for the griddle, fully open the valve on the propane tank to allow the gas to flow freely. Next, adjust the control knob to the 'light' position, which gets the gas flowing to the ignition source. Hit the ignition button to create a spark that ignites the gas. If the griddle doesn't light up within a few seconds, it's crucial to turn off the gas supply right away to prevent unburned gas from building up, which could lead to flare-ups. Give it a few minutes for any leftover gas to disperse in the air before attempting to ignite the griddle again.

Being able to adjust the flame accurately can significantly impact your cooking results. The control knobs on the griddle are designed for fine-tuning heat management, allowing for precise adjustments to the flame intensity. If you're new to griddle cooking, starting with a medium flame setting is a good idea, as it provides a balanced environment to see how the griddle responds to different heat levels. As you gain experience, you'll develop an intuitive sense of the specific flame settings needed to achieve the ideal cooking temperatures for a variety of foods, from searing meats to gently cooking vegetables.

Investing in the right accessories can greatly enhance the functionality and versatility of your Blackstone Griddle. A sturdy griddle cover is recommended to protect it from environmental elements, especially if you'll be storing the griddle outdoors. A hard cover is preferable due to its superior durability and enhanced protection against precipitation like rain and snow, compared to a soft cover. Additionally, a grease management tool is essential for keeping a clean cooking surface and minimizing the risk of flare-ups caused by excess grease. Effective grease management involves regularly scraping excess grease into the designated grease trap and ensuring that the trap is emptied promptly after each cooking session.

Carrying out seasonal maintenance is crucial for the longevity and performance of your griddle. Before storing the griddle for extended periods, such as during winter, it's important to conduct a thorough cleaning and apply a fresh layer of oil to the cooking surface. This acts as a barrier against moisture, helping to prevent rust and corrosion. For those living in areas where outdoor grilling is possible year-round, it's still essential to perform periodic inspections and maintenance tasks to keep the griddle in top shape.

Addressing common operational issues through troubleshooting can help prevent unnecessary downtime and reduce frustration. If you notice uneven heating across the griddle surface, it's wise to check the burner tubes for any blockages or debris that could hinder gas flow. Also, ensure the propane tank and its connections are in good condition. A low flame or trouble lighting the griddle often signals a problem with the propane supply or the regulator, which may need resetting or, in some cases, replacement to restore proper functionality.

Setting Up for the First Time

Unboxing your Blackstone Griddle marks the beginning of an exciting culinary adventure. Start by carefully assembling the unit following the detailed instructions provided by the manufacturer. Each component, from the griddle plate to the burner assembly, needs to be perfectly aligned and securely fastened. This careful attention to detail ensures that the assembled unit remains stable and structurally sound during operation, which helps to avoid any potential hazards or interruptions.

Choosing the right spot for your griddle is crucial. It's essential to place it on a level surface made of non-combustible materials, such as concrete or stone, to reduce fire risks. The selected location should be kept at a safe distance from flammable items, including wooden structures, overhanging branches, or other combustible materials. Since the griddle is powered by propane, it's also important to set it up in an area with good ventilation. This step is necessary to prevent the buildup of propane gas fumes, which could create a serious safety concern.

Before you fire up the griddle for the first time, take a close look at the propane tank and its connections. Start by checking the outside of the propane tank for any signs of damage, like dents, rust, or corrosion, which could suggest potential leaks. Next, inspect the hose and regulator assembly, ensuring the connections are secure and free from deformities, such as kinks or blockages, that could restrict gas flow. This thorough check is vital for both safety and ensuring a consistent gas supply to the griddle.

Seasoning the griddle top is a key step in getting it ready for optimal performance. Begin this process by heating the griddle to a high temperature, ensuring even heat across the entire surface. Once it reaches the desired temperature, apply a thin, uniform layer of oil with a high smoke point, such as flaxseed or canola oil, over the entire cooking surface. This should be done carefully for complete coverage to promote the polymerization process. The oil undergoes a chemical transformation, creating a strong, protective coating that prevents rust and establishes a non-stick surface ideal for cooking. Repeat this seasoning process several times, allowing the griddle to cool slightly between applications, to build a durable and long-lasting seasoning layer.

With the griddle seasoned and ready, it's time to ignite it for the first time. Start by cautiously opening the propane valve, letting the gas flow slowly. Turn the ignition knob to the 'light' position while pressing the ignition button to create a spark that ignites the gas. Pay attention to the flame's characteristics, especially its color and intensity. A steady, predominantly blue flame indicates an optimal gas-to-air ratio, meaning the griddle is getting the right amount of gas and is ready for cooking. Adjust the flame intensity as needed to achieve the exact temperature required for your culinary creations.

Essential Grilling Tools

Delving into the intricacies of Blackstone grilling becomes significantly more engaging and efficient when equipped with the right tools and accessories specifically designed to streamline the cooking process and enhance the culinary experience. These thoughtfully chosen items not only facilitate the execution of various cooking techniques but also ensure that each dish prepared on the griddle showcases a high level of skill and finesse. A high-quality metal spatula is indispensable due to its multifunctionality, allowing for seamless flipping of burgers, precise stir-frying of vegetables, and thorough cleaning of the griddle surface. When selecting a spatula, prioritize those with ergonomically designed handles that offer a solid grip, complemented by a flexible yet sturdy stainless steel blade that provides both control and durability, ensuring longevity and improved performance during grilling sessions.

A pair of long-handled tongs is an essential tool for ensuring precision and safety while handling food items on the griddle. These tongs enable you to manipulate food without the risk of burns, which is crucial when dealing with delicate items such as fish fillets or slender asparagus spears. In choosing the right tongs, it is vital to consider the quality of the grip, the ease of maneuverability, and their resistance to high temperatures. Opt for tongs with silicone or rubber-coated handles that enhance comfort and provide a secure hold, minimizing the risk of slippage even when working with greasy or slippery foods.

For those aspiring to master the art of Blackstone grilling, incorporating a basting cover can be a game-changer. This dome-shaped accessory is designed to facilitate even and accelerated cooking, making it particularly useful for tasks such as melting cheese evenly over burgers or steaming vegetables to perfection. It works by trapping heat and moisture, intensifying flavors and reducing cooking times, which adds a professional touch to your grilling repertoire.

The maintenance of your griddle's cooking surface is critically dependent on using a robust griddle scraper, specifically engineered for Blackstone equipment. This tool is instrumental in efficiently removing food residues and excess grease while also aiding in the even distribution of oils during the seasoning process. When selecting a scraper, it's important to choose one with a comfortable handle for prolonged use and a blade that matches the width of your griddle for comprehensive cleaning coverage.

Investing in a digital meat thermometer is essential for achieving precise cooking results with meats, ensuring they reach the desired level of doneness consistently. This device eliminates the uncertainty associated with grilling, making it a valuable asset for both novice and seasoned grillers. The thermometer provides accurate readings that allow for meticulous monitoring of internal meat temperatures, guaranteeing culinary excellence and safety in every grilling endeavor.

Basic Techniques and Tips

To achieve exceptional results with the Blackstone Griddle, it's essential to refine specific techniques that can significantly boost your grilling skills. Mastering temperature control is crucial. The Blackstone Griddle features a wide range of temperature settings, enabling both intense searing and gentle cooking. Take the time to familiarize yourself with the nuances of the low, medium, and high temperature settings. For most types of meat, a medium-high heat setting is ideal for achieving a perfect sear on the outside while keeping the inside just right. On the other hand, vegetables and more delicate proteins like fish benefit from being cooked at medium to medium-low heat to maintain their texture and flavor.

Utilizing the method of zone cooking is incredibly beneficial. The Blackstone's large cooking surface offers plenty of space for various food items, each needing different temperature levels. Make strategic use of the griddle's hotter areas to achieve an excellent sear on meats, while saving the cooler sections for cooking vegetables or keeping items like buns warm. This approach not only boosts efficiency but also ensures that everything is served at its best temperature.

The preparatory steps before cooking are vital for achieving top-notch results. Allowing meats to come to room temperature before grilling is important, as this aids in even cooking. Additionally, patting the meat dry is crucial to eliminate excess moisture, which can hinder the creation of a nice crust. A light coating of oil serves two purposes: it reduces the risk of sticking to the griddle and helps develop a beautifully browned crust.

Careful handling of food on the griddle is essential. Use a sharp, thin spatula for the delicate task of flipping burgers or fragile items like fish fillets. It's best to avoid flipping meats too soon; instead, wait until they naturally release from the griddle, signaling that a proper sear has been achieved.

Allowing meat to rest after cooking is a key step that enables juices to redistribute throughout, enhancing its moisture and flavor. A good rule of thumb is to let the meat rest for about five minutes for each inch of thickness, ensuring optimal juiciness and flavor retention.

Thorough cleaning and maintenance of the griddle should be performed after each use. While the griddle is still warm, quickly scrape off any leftover food particles and wipe the surface with a paper towel. Applying a thin layer of oil after cleaning is crucial to prevent rust and maintain the seasoning of the griddle, setting it up for your next grilling adventure.

Preheating and Temperature Control

Initiate the preheating process for your Blackstone Griddle by igniting the burners and adjusting them to your preferred setting, making sure the cooking surface reaches a nice, even temperature. This step is key for achieving consistent cooking results across the entire surface area, which is especially important for getting that perfect Maillard reaction on proteins. Allow about 10 to 15 minutes for the griddle to hit the necessary temperature. For high-heat tasks, like searing steaks or burgers, set your griddle to a medium-high thermal setting. This adjustment should help you reach surface temperatures around 400°F to 450°F. Such a temperature range is perfect for creating a delicious caramelized crust on your meats while keeping the inside juicy and tender.

When you're preparing more delicate items, like eggs or pancakes, it's best to choose a medium thermal setting. This will help the griddle stabilize at temperatures between 350°F and 375°F. Staying within this range is crucial to prevent charring on the outer layers and ensures that the food is evenly cooked throughout, maintaining its texture and moisture.

Mastering the thermal zones on your Blackstone Griddle can greatly elevate your cooking skills. The griddle's surface may show varying thermal intensities, which you can strategically use with the zone cooking technique. By managing different sections of your griddle at various temperatures, you can prepare a variety of foods at the same time. Reserve the higher-temperature zones for searing meats while using the lower-temperature areas for tasks like toasting buns or cooking delicate vegetables.

In addition to temperature control, choosing the right cooking oil is essential. Go for oils with a high smoke point, like avocado oil or canola oil, to reduce the chance of smoking and burning during high-heat cooking. These oils not only create a cleaner cooking environment but also enhance the flavor of your dishes.

Keep in mind that environmental factors, such as ambient temperature and wind, can significantly affect your griddle's thermal dynamics. On colder or windy days, you may need to crank up the burner output to maintain your desired cooking temperature. Conversely, on hot days with little wind, you might need to dial down the burner to avoid overheating.

Using an infrared thermometer can greatly improve the accuracy of your grilling. This handy tool lets you measure the surface temperature of your griddle at various spots, ensuring that each food item is cooked at its ideal temperature. This level of precise control is vital for avoiding undercooked or overcooked meals.

Cleaning and Maintenance

To maintain your Blackstone Griddle in optimal working condition, it's essential to engage in a regular cleaning and upkeep routine. This practice, carried out after each use, is crucial for preventing debris buildup and rust, ensuring that your griddle is always ready for your next outdoor cooking adventure.

Start the cleaning process by letting the griddle cool down to a safe, moderate temperature after cooking. A surface that's still slightly warm helps loosen residual food particles, making it easier to clean and minimizing the risk of burns during handling.

Use a metal scraper or spatula to carefully dislodge and remove any food particles or residue stuck to the griddle's surface. This step is vital to avoid the accumulation of charred remnants, which can negatively impact the griddle's performance and the flavor of your future meals.

After scraping, cleanse the griddle surface with a damp cloth or paper towel. For spots where residue remains stubborn, add a little water directly onto the warm surface. This method helps to loosen tough deposits. It's best to avoid using soap unless absolutely necessary, as it can disrupt the seasoning layer that protects the griddle's surface.

Since moisture can lead to rust on materials like cast iron and steel, it's important to thoroughly dry the griddle surface with a clean cloth or paper towels after cleaning. If possible, apply heat to the griddle for a short time to ensure any leftover moisture evaporates.

Once dried, apply a thin, even layer of cooking oil to the griddle surface. This serves two purposes: protecting the surface and maintaining its non-stick qualities. Choose oils with a high smoke point, such as canola, vegetable, or flaxseed oil. Spread the oil evenly across the surface using a paper towel, then heat the griddle until the oil starts to smoke. Turn off the heat and let the griddle cool down. This process replenishes the seasoning and creates a protective barrier against rust.

After cooling and completing the seasoning process, protect your griddle from environmental elements by covering it, especially if it's stored outdoors. This simple step helps prevent moisture buildup and reduces the risk of rust.

Regularly inspect your griddle for any early signs of rust. If you spot any, remove it with a metal scraper or fine-grit sandpaper. Clean the affected area, ensure it's completely dry, and reapply seasoning to restore the protective coating.

For storage, it's best to keep your Blackstone Griddle in a dry, covered location to limit exposure to moisture. If indoor storage isn't an option, make sure the outdoor cover fits securely and check periodically for signs of moisture or physical damage.

Chapter 2: 30 Breakfast Recipes

1. Pancake Stack with Maple Syrup

Portion Size: 2

Duration: 25 minutes

Ingredients:

- 1 cup all-purpose flour
- 2 tablespoons granulated sugar
- 1 tablespoon baking powder
- 1/4 teaspoon salt
- 1 cup milk
- 2 tablespoons unsalted butter, melted, plus more for greasing the griddle
- 1 large egg
- 1 teaspoon vanilla extract
- Pure maple syrup, for serving
- Fresh berries (optional), for serving

Instructions:

1. **Preheat the Blackstone Griddle** over medium heat. You'll want it to reach a temperature of around 375°F (190°C) for optimal pancake cooking.

2. **Mix Dry Ingredients:** In a large bowl, whisk together the flour, sugar, baking powder, and salt until well combined.

3. **Combine Wet Ingredients:** In a separate bowl, beat the milk, melted butter, egg, and vanilla extract until the mixture is smooth.

4. **Combine Wet and Dry Ingredients:** Pour the wet ingredients into the dry ingredients. Stir until just combined; it's okay if the batter is a little lumpy. Overmixing can make the pancakes tough.

5. **Grease the Griddle:** Lightly brush the griddle with melted butter. This will prevent the pancakes from sticking and give them a golden-brown exterior.

6. **Cook the Pancakes:** Pour 1/4 cup of batter onto the griddle for each pancake. Cook until bubbles form on the surface and the edges look set, about 2 to 3 minutes. Flip with a spatula and cook for another 2 minutes on the other side, or until golden brown.

7. **Serve Immediately:** Stack the pancakes on plates. Drizzle generously with pure maple syrup and, if desired, top with fresh berries.

8. **Repeat:** Continue with the remaining batter, adding more butter to the griddle as needed. Depending on the size of your griddle, you can cook multiple pancakes at once to serve everyone hot, delicious pancakes at the same time.

Remember, the key to perfect pancakes on the Blackstone Griddle is maintaining the right temperature and lightly greasing the surface before each batch. Enjoy your pancake stack with the rich flavor of maple syrup and the optional freshness of berries for a delightful breakfast experience.

2. Breakfast Burrito with Sausage and Eggs

Portion Size: 2

Duration: 25 minutes

Ingredients:

- 4 large eggs
- 1/2 lb ground sausage
- 2 large flour tortillas
- 1/2 cup shredded cheddar cheese
- 1/4 cup diced onion
- 1/4 cup diced bell pepper
- Salt and pepper to taste
- 2 tablespoons olive oil
- Optional toppings: salsa, sour cream, avocado slices

Instructions:

1. **Preheat the Blackstone Griddle** over medium heat. Ensure it reaches a consistent temperature before adding ingredients.

2. **Cook the Sausage**: Place the ground sausage on the griddle. Use a spatula to break it apart into smaller pieces. Cook for about 5-7 minutes or until fully browned. Once cooked, transfer the sausage to a plate and set aside.

3. **Sauté Vegetables**: In the same area where you cooked the sausage, add the diced onion and bell pepper. Sauté for 3-4 minutes, or until the vegetables are soft and slightly caramelized. Remove from the griddle and mix them with the cooked sausage.

4. **Scramble the Eggs**: Crack the eggs into a bowl, add salt and pepper, and beat them until well mixed. Add a tablespoon of olive oil to a clean section of the griddle. Pour in the eggs and let them sit for a moment before gently scrambling them with a spatula. Cook until the eggs are firm but still moist, about 2-3 minutes.

5. **Warm the Tortillas**: Place the flour tortillas on the griddle for about 30 seconds on each side, just until they are warm and pliable.

6. **Assemble the Burritos**: On each tortilla, layer an equal amount of the scrambled eggs, sausage and vegetable mixture, and shredded cheddar cheese. Add any optional toppings you prefer.

7. **Roll the Burritos**: Fold the bottom of the tortilla up over the filling, then fold in the sides and roll tightly to close. For a crispy finish, place the rolled burritos seam-side down on the griddle for 1-2 minutes, or until golden brown and the cheese has melted.

8. **Serve Immediately**: Cut the burritos in half, if desired, and serve hot with additional toppings on the side.

Enjoy a delicious start to your day with these easy and flavorful Breakfast Burritos, perfectly cooked on your Blackstone Griddle.

3. Griddled French Toast with Berries

Portion Size: 2

⏳ Duration: 30 minutes

🛒 Ingredients:

- 4 slices of thick-cut bread (preferably brioche or challah)
- 2 large eggs
- 1/2 cup whole milk
- 1/4 cup heavy cream
- 2 tablespoons granulated sugar
- 1 teaspoon vanilla extract
- 1/2 teaspoon ground cinnamon
- Pinch of salt
- 2 tablespoons unsalted butter, for griddling
- 1 cup mixed berries (such as strawberries, blueberries, and raspberries)
- Powdered sugar, for dusting
- Maple syrup, for serving

👨‍🍳 Instructions:

1. **Preheat the Blackstone Griddle** to medium heat, around 350°F (175°C). It's crucial to allow the griddle to fully preheat to ensure even cooking.

2. **Prepare the French toast batter** by whisking together the eggs, whole milk, heavy cream, granulated sugar, vanilla extract, ground cinnamon, and a pinch of salt in a shallow dish. Mix until well combined and smooth.

3. **Dip the bread slices** into the batter, allowing each side to soak for about 30 seconds. Avoid soaking for too long to prevent the bread from becoming too soggy.

4. **Melt the butter on the griddle**, spreading it evenly over the cooking surface. This will help to prevent sticking and add a rich flavor to the French toast.

5. **Place the soaked bread slices on the griddle**, leaving some space between each slice. Cook for about 4-5 minutes on each side or until golden brown and crispy. The key is to not move the bread around too much once it's on the griddle to achieve a nice, even crust.

6. **While the French toast is cooking**, gently toss the mixed berries in a small bowl. This is a good time to prepare any other sides or toppings you'll be serving.

7. **Serve the French toast hot** off the griddle, topped with the fresh mixed berries. Dust with powdered sugar and drizzle with maple syrup to taste.

8. **Adjust the griddle temperature** as needed. If the bread is browning too quickly, turn the heat down slightly. Conversely, if it's not browning enough, increase the heat. The goal is to achieve a perfect balance of crispy exterior and soft, custardy interior.

9. **Enjoy immediately**. French toast is best served fresh and hot for the ultimate breakfast experience.

4. Crispy Bacon and Egg Sandwich

Portion Size: 2

⏳ Duration: 20 minutes

🛒 Ingredients:

- 4 slices of thick-cut bacon
- 2 large eggs
- 2 tablespoons of unsalted butter, divided
- 4 slices of sourdough bread
- 2 slices of cheddar cheese
- Salt and pepper, to taste
- Optional: sliced avocado or tomato for added freshness

📝 Instructions:

1. Preheat your Blackstone griddle to medium-high heat, around 375°F (190°C).

2. Lay the bacon slices on the griddle. Cook for about 4-5 minutes per side, or until crispy. Transfer the bacon to a paper towel-lined plate to drain excess grease.

3. Reduce the griddle heat to medium. In the same griddle area used for bacon, crack the eggs and cook for about 2-3 minutes for a soft yolk or 4-5 minutes for a firmer yolk. Season with salt and pepper to taste.

4. While the eggs are cooking, spread 1 tablespoon of butter on one side of each slice of sourdough bread. Place the bread, buttered side down, on another area of the griddle to toast. Cook for about 2 minutes or until golden brown, then flip to toast the other side lightly.

5. Assemble the sandwich: On two slices of toasted bread, layer a slice of cheddar cheese, two slices of crispy bacon, and a fried egg. If using, add sliced avocado or tomato on top of the egg before closing the sandwich with the other slices of toasted bread.

6. With the remaining tablespoon of butter, lightly butter the griddle and place the assembled sandwiches back on it. Press down gently with a spatula to ensure the cheese melts and the sandwich heats through, about 1-2 minutes per side.

7. Serve immediately while hot and crispy. Enjoy your Crispy Bacon and Egg Sandwich straight off the Blackstone griddle, perfect for a hearty and satisfying breakfast.

5. Griddle-Cooked Hash Browns

🍽 Portion Size: 2

⏳ Duration: 30 minutes

🛒 Ingredients:
- 2 large russet potatoes, peeled
- 2 tablespoons unsalted butter, melted
- Salt, to taste
- Black pepper, to taste
- Optional: 1/4 cup finely chopped onion for added flavor

📝 Instructions:

1. **Preparation of Potatoes**: Begin by grating the peeled russet potatoes using the large holes of a box grater. To remove excess moisture, place the grated potatoes in a clean kitchen towel and squeeze out as much liquid as possible. This step is crucial for achieving crispy hash browns.

2. **Seasoning**: Transfer the dried grated potatoes to a mixing bowl. If you're using onions, add them here. Pour the melted butter over the potatoes, and season generously with salt and black pepper. Toss everything together to ensure the potatoes are evenly coated with butter and seasoning.

3. **Preheating the Griddle**: Heat your Blackstone griddle over medium-high heat. Allow it to come to temperature, which usually takes about 5 minutes. A properly preheated griddle is key to cooking the hash browns evenly and achieving a golden crust.

4. **Cooking the Hash Browns**: Once the griddle is hot, divide the potato mixture into two portions on the griddle. Flatten each portion with a spatula to form a thin layer, about 1/2 inch thick. Cook without disturbing for about 5-7 minutes, or until the bottom is golden brown and crispy.

5. **Flipping**: Carefully flip the hash browns using a wide spatula. Cook for another 5-7 minutes on the other side, or until it is also golden brown and crispy. Adjust the heat if necessary to prevent burning.

6. **Serving**: Once both sides of the hash browns are crispy and golden, transfer them to a plate lined with paper towels to absorb any excess grease. Serve immediately while hot and crispy for the best texture and flavor.

By following these detailed steps, you'll enjoy perfectly crispy, golden hash browns cooked on your Blackstone griddle. This simple yet delicious breakfast side dish is a great way to start your day or complement any meal.

6. *Blueberry Pancakes with Lemon Zest*

Portion Size: Serves 2

Duration: 25 minutes

Ingredients:

- 1 cup all-purpose flour
- 2 tablespoons sugar
- 1 tablespoon baking powder
- 1/4 teaspoon salt
- Zest of 1 lemon
- 1 cup milk
- 1 egg
- 2 tablespoons unsalted butter, melted, plus more for greasing the griddle
- 1 teaspoon vanilla extract
- 1 cup fresh blueberries
- Maple syrup, for serving

Instructions:

1. **Preheat the Blackstone Griddle** to medium heat (around 350°F). Lightly grease the surface with butter.

2. **Mix Dry Ingredients**: In a large bowl, whisk together the flour, sugar, baking powder, salt, and lemon zest.

3. **Combine Wet Ingredients**: In a separate bowl, beat the milk, egg, melted butter, and vanilla extract until well combined.

4. **Combine Wet and Dry Ingredients**: Make a well in the center of the dry ingredients and pour in the wet ingredients. Stir until just combined; do not overmix. The batter should have small lumps.

5. **Fold in Blueberries**: Gently fold the blueberries into the batter, ensuring they are evenly distributed.

6. **Cook the Pancakes**: Pour 1/4 cup of batter for each pancake onto the preheated griddle. Cook until bubbles form on the surface and the edges look set, about 2-3 minutes. Flip with a spatula and cook for another 2 minutes or until golden brown and cooked through.

7. **Serve Warm**: Serve the pancakes hot off the griddle with a generous drizzle of maple syrup.

Note: For best results, avoid pressing down on the pancakes with the spatula after flipping, as this can deflate them. Enjoy your fluffy, flavorful blueberry pancakes with the delightful zest of lemon for a perfect start to your day!

7. *Grilled Banana and Nutella Wrap*

Portion Size: 2

Duration: 15 minutes

Ingredients:

- 2 large flour tortillas
- 4 tablespoons Nutella (or any chocolate hazelnut spread)
- 2 bananas, peeled and sliced lengthwise
- 1 tablespoon butter, for grilling
- Optional toppings: powdered sugar, whipped cream, or cinnamon

Instructions:

1. **Preheat the Blackstone Griddle** over medium heat. Aim for a surface temperature of around 350°F (175°C) to ensure your wraps cook evenly without burning.

2. **Prepare the Wraps**: Lay out the flour tortillas on a flat surface. Spread 2 tablespoons of Nutella on each tortilla, leaving a small border around the edges to prevent it from oozing out when melted.

3. **Add the Bananas**: Place the sliced bananas on one half of each tortilla, arranging them in a single layer over the Nutella.

4. **Fold the Wraps**: Carefully fold the tortillas in half over the bananas, pressing gently to seal the Nutella and bananas inside.

5. **Grill the Wraps**: Add a tablespoon of butter to the griddle and allow it to melt, spreading it evenly over the cooking surface. Place the folded wraps on the griddle and cook for about 2-3 minutes on each side, or until they are golden brown and crispy. The Nutella will become warm and gooey.

6. **Serve Immediately**: Once cooked, transfer the wraps to a cutting board. If desired, slice each wrap in half to make them easier to eat. Serve hot, garnished with optional toppings like a dusting of powdered sugar, a dollop of whipped cream, or a sprinkle of cinnamon for an extra flavor boost.

7. **Enjoy Your Grilled Banana and Nutella Wrap**: Dive into this deliciously warm and gooey treat right off the griddle. Perfect for a quick breakfast, a sweet snack, or a dessert that combines the comfort of grilled tortillas with the irresistible duo of Nutella and banana.

8. Classic Eggs Benedict on the Griddle

Portion Size: 2

Duration: 30 minutes

Ingredients:

- 4 large eggs (for poaching)
- 2 English muffins, split
- 4 slices of Canadian bacon
- 1 tablespoon white vinegar (for poaching eggs)
- 1 teaspoon salt (for poaching water)
- For the Hollandaise Sauce:
  - 3 egg yolks
  - 1 tablespoon lemon juice
  - 1/2 cup unsalted butter, melted
  - Pinch of cayenne pepper
  - Salt, to taste

Instructions:

1. **Preheat the Blackstone Griddle** to medium heat (around 375°F). Lightly oil the surface.

2. **Prepare the Hollandaise Sauce:**
   - In a blender, combine 3 egg yolks, 1 tablespoon of lemon juice, a pinch of cayenne pepper, and a pinch of salt. Blend on high speed until the mixture lightens in color, about 20-30 seconds.
   - With the blender running on low speed, slowly drizzle in 1/2 cup of melted butter until the sauce thickens. Set aside in a warm place.

3. **Poach the Eggs:**
   - Fill a shallow pan with about 3 inches of water. Add 1 tablespoon of white vinegar and 1 teaspoon of salt. Bring to a gentle simmer over medium heat.
   - Crack an egg into a small bowl. Gently slide the egg into the simmering water. Repeat with the remaining eggs. Poach for about 3-4 minutes or until the whites are set but yolks remain runny. Use a slotted spoon to remove the eggs and set them on a warm plate.

4. **Cook the Canadian Bacon and English Muffins:**
   - Place the Canadian bacon slices on the preheated griddle. Cook for about 2 minutes per side or until lightly browned. Transfer to a plate.
   - Place the English muffin halves, cut side down, on the griddle. Toast for about 1-2 minutes or until golden brown.

5. **Assemble the Eggs Benedict:**
   - Place two toasted English muffin halves on each plate. Top each half with a slice of Canadian bacon.
   - Carefully place a poached egg on top of each bacon slice.
   - Generously spoon the Hollandaise sauce over the eggs.
   - Serve immediately, garnished with a pinch of cayenne pepper or chopped chives if desired.

Following these steps will help you create a classic Eggs Benedict on your Blackstone Griddle, perfect for a luxurious breakfast or brunch. Enjoy the creamy Hollandaise, the richness of the poached egg, and the savory Canadian bacon atop a crispy English muffin, all brought together with the ease and joy of griddle cooking.

9. Griddle-Seared Avocado Toast

Portion Size: 2

Duration: 15 minutes

Ingredients:

- 4 slices of sourdough bread
- 2 ripe avocados
- 1 tablespoon olive oil
- 1 teaspoon lime juice
- Salt and pepper to taste
- 1 small radish, thinly sliced
- 1/4 cup crumbled feta cheese
- 2 tablespoons chopped cilantro
- Red pepper flakes (optional)

Instructions:

1. **Preheat the Blackstone Griddle** over medium heat. Ensure the surface is clean and lightly greased with a bit of olive oil to prevent sticking.

2. **Prepare the Avocado Mixture:** In a small bowl, mash the avocados with a fork until they reach a slightly chunky consistency. Stir in the lime juice, salt, and pepper. Adjust the seasoning according to your taste.

3. **Griddle the Sourdough:** Brush each slice of sourdough bread lightly with olive oil. Place the bread slices on the hot griddle and cook for about 2 minutes on each side, or until they are nicely toasted and have grill marks.

4. **Assemble the Avocado Toast:** Spread the mashed avocado evenly over the toasted sourdough slices. Top each slice with a few radish slices, a sprinkle of crumbled feta cheese, and a bit of chopped cilantro for freshness. If you like a bit of heat, add a few red pepper flakes over the top.

5. **Serve Immediately:** Enjoy your Griddle-Seared Avocado Toast while it's warm and the bread is still crispy. This dish pairs wonderfully with a side of grilled tomatoes or a fresh green salad for a complete breakfast.

By following these steps, you'll have a delicious and visually appealing breakfast that showcases the versatility and ease of cooking with your Blackstone Griddle.

10. Cheddar and Chive Omelette

Portion Size: 2

Duration: 15 minutes

Ingredients:

- 4 large eggs
- 1/4 cup milk

- 1/2 cup shredded cheddar cheese
- 2 tablespoons fresh chives, finely chopped
- Salt and pepper, to taste
- 1 tablespoon unsalted butter

Instructions:

1. **Preheat the Blackstone Griddle:** Turn your Blackstone Griddle to medium heat and allow it to preheat for about 5 minutes. A properly preheated griddle ensures even cooking and prevents the omelette from sticking.

2. **Mix the Eggs:** In a medium bowl, whisk together the eggs, milk, salt, and pepper until well combined and slightly frothy. This introduces air into the eggs, making the omelette fluffier.

3. **Add Butter:** Once the griddle is hot, add the butter and swirl it around to coat the surface. The butter not only adds flavor but also helps in achieving that golden-brown exterior on the omelette.

4. **Cook the Egg Mixture:** Pour the egg mixture onto the griddle, forming a large circle. Let it cook undisturbed for about 1 minute or until the edges start to set. The gentle heat allows the omelette to cook evenly without browning too quickly.

5. **Add Cheese and Chives:** Sprinkle the shredded cheddar cheese and chopped chives over half of the omelette. The cheese should start melting from the residual heat, while the chives add a fresh, oniony flavor.

6. **Fold the Omelette:** Once the bottom of the omelette is set but the top is still slightly runny, use a spatula to carefully fold it in half over the cheese and chives. This traps the heat inside, ensuring the cheese melts beautifully and the omelette cooks through.

7. **Final Cook:** Let the omelette cook for another 1-2 minutes, or until fully set and the cheese inside has melted. Adjust the heat if necessary to prevent the bottom from burning.

8. **Serve:** Carefully slide the omelette onto a plate. The omelette should be fluffy, with a slightly creamy center from the melted cheese. Serve immediately for the best experience.

By following these steps, you'll create a delicious Cheddar and Chive Omelette on your Blackstone Griddle that's perfect for a quick, satisfying breakfast. Enjoy the ease of griddle cooking with this simple yet flavorful recipe.

11. Cinnamon Roll Pancakes

Portion Size: 2

Duration: 30 minutes

Ingredients:

- 1 cup all-purpose flour
- 2 tablespoons granulated sugar
- 1/2 teaspoon baking powder
- 1/2 teaspoon baking soda
- 1/4 teaspoon salt
- 3/4 cup buttermilk
- 1 large egg
- 2 tablespoons unsalted butter, melted
- 1 teaspoon vanilla extract

- **Cinnamon Swirl:**
  - 1/4 cup unsalted butter, melted
  - 1/3 cup brown sugar
  - 1 tablespoon ground cinnamon
- **Cream Cheese Glaze:**
  - 4 ounces cream cheese, softened
  - 1/4 cup powdered sugar
  - 1/2 teaspoon vanilla extract
  - 2 to 3 tablespoons milk

Instructions:

1. **Prepare the Pancake Batter:**
   - In a large bowl, whisk together the flour, granulated sugar, baking powder, baking soda, and salt.
   - In another bowl, combine the buttermilk, egg, melted butter, and vanilla extract.
   - Pour the wet ingredients into the dry ingredients and stir until just combined. Be careful not to overmix; a few lumps are okay.

2. **Make the Cinnamon Swirl:**
   - In a small bowl, mix together the melted butter, brown sugar, and ground cinnamon until well combined.
   - Transfer the mixture to a squeeze bottle or a zip-top bag with a small corner snipped off.

3. **Prepare the Cream Cheese Glaze:**
   - In a medium bowl, beat together the cream cheese, powdered sugar, and vanilla extract.
   - Gradually add milk, one tablespoon at a time, until the glaze reaches a pourable consistency.

4. **Cook the Pancakes:**
   - Preheat the Blackstone griddle to medium-low heat and lightly grease with butter or oil.
   - Pour 1/4 cup of batter onto the griddle for each pancake. Allow to cook until bubbles form on the surface, about 2 minutes.
   - Before flipping, squeeze the cinnamon swirl mixture in a spiral pattern onto the top of each pancake.
   - Flip the pancakes carefully and cook for an additional 1-2 minutes, or until golden brown and cooked through.

5. **Serve:**
   - Serve the pancakes hot with a generous drizzle of the cream cheese glaze.

Note: For the best results, ensure your griddle is at the correct temperature before starting to cook the pancakes. This will prevent them from sticking and ensure they cook evenly.

12. Smoked Salmon and Cream Cheese Bagel

Portion Size: 2

Duration: 15 minutes

Ingredients:

- 2 plain bagels, halved
- 4 oz cream cheese, softened
- 4 oz smoked salmon
- 1 small red onion, thinly sliced
- 1 tablespoon capers, drained

- 2 tablespoons fresh dill, chopped
- 1 tablespoon olive oil
- Freshly ground black pepper, to taste

Instructions:

1. Preheat your Blackstone griddle to medium heat. Brush the griddle lightly with olive oil to prevent the bagels from sticking.

2. Place the bagel halves cut side down onto the griddle. Toast them for about 2-3 minutes or until they are golden brown and crispy. Remove the bagels from the griddle and set them aside.

3. Spread a generous amount of cream cheese on the cut side of each bagel half.

4. Layer slices of smoked salmon over the cream cheese on each bagel half.

5. Sprinkle the thinly sliced red onion, capers, and fresh dill evenly over the smoked salmon.

6. Season with freshly ground black pepper to taste.

7. Serve immediately while the bagels are still warm and enjoy a delicious, griddle-made breakfast.

13. Griddled Breakfast Quesadilla

Portion Size: 2

Duration: 20 minutes

Ingredients:

- 4 large eggs
- 1/4 cup milk
- Salt and pepper, to taste
- 1 tablespoon olive oil
- 1/2 cup cooked and crumbled breakfast sausage
- 1/2 cup shredded cheddar cheese
- 1/4 cup diced green bell pepper
- 1/4 cup diced red onion
- 2 large flour tortillas
- Salsa, for serving
- Sour cream, for serving

Instructions:

1. **Preheat the Blackstone Griddle** over medium heat. Ensure it reaches a consistent temperature before starting to cook.

2. **Whisk the Eggs:** In a medium bowl, beat the eggs with the milk, salt, and pepper until well combined.

3. **Cook the Vegetables:** Add half the olive oil to the griddle. Sauté the green bell pepper and red onion for about 2-3 minutes, or until they start to soften. Remove from the griddle and set aside.

4. **Scramble the Eggs:** Add the remaining olive oil to the griddle. Pour in the egg mixture and allow it to set for a few seconds. Gently scramble the eggs, pushing them from the edges towards the center until they are softly set. Remove from the griddle and set aside with the vegetables.

5. **Assemble the Quesadillas:** Lay out the flour tortillas on a flat surface. On one half of each tortilla, evenly distribute the scrambled eggs, cooked vegetables, crumbled breakfast sausage, and shredded cheddar cheese.

6. **Fold and Cook:** Fold the tortillas in half over the filling to create a half-moon shape. Place the quesadillas on the griddle and cook for about 2-3 minutes on each side, or until golden brown and the cheese has melted.

7. **Serve:** Cut each quesadilla into wedges and serve with salsa and sour cream on the side.

This Griddled Breakfast Quesadilla recipe combines the ease of Blackstone griddle cooking with the delicious flavors of a hearty breakfast, making it a perfect meal to start your day.

14. Spinach and Feta Omelette

Portion Size: 2

Duration: 20 minutes

Ingredients:

- 4 large eggs
- 1/4 cup milk
- 1/2 cup fresh spinach, chopped
- 1/2 cup feta cheese, crumbled
- 1/4 teaspoon salt
- 1/4 teaspoon black pepper
- 1 tablespoon olive oil
- 2 tablespoons red onion, finely chopped
- 1 clove garlic, minced

Instructions:

1. **Preparation**: In a medium bowl, whisk together the eggs, milk, salt, and pepper until well combined. Set aside.

2. **Preheat the Griddle**: Turn your Blackstone griddle to medium heat and allow it to preheat for about 5 minutes. The ideal temperature for cooking omelettes is around 375°F (190°C).

3. **Cook the Filling**: Add the olive oil to the griddle, followed by the chopped red onion and minced garlic. Sauté for 2-3 minutes until the onions are translucent and fragrant. Add the chopped spinach and cook for an additional 1-2 minutes until the spinach is wilted. Transfer the filling to a plate and set aside.

4. **Cook the Omelette**: Pour the egg mixture onto the griddle, forming a large circle. Cook for 1-2 minutes until the edges start to firm up. Using a spatula, gently lift the edges of the omelette, allowing the uncooked egg to flow underneath.

5. **Add Filling and Feta**: Once the top of the omelette is almost set but still slightly runny, sprinkle the cooked spinach mixture and crumbled feta cheese over one half of the omelette.

6. **Fold and Serve**: Carefully fold the other half of the omelette over the filling. Let it cook for another minute to ensure the feta is slightly melted. Using a spatula, gently slide the omelette onto a plate.

7. **Finishing Touches**: Cut the omelette in half to create two portions. Serve immediately for the best taste and texture experience.

This Spinach and Feta Omelette, cooked on your Blackstone griddle, combines the ease of outdoor cooking with the sophistication of a classic breakfast favorite. Enjoy the seamless blend of flavors and the joy of griddle cooking!

15. Griddled Corned Beef Hash

Portion Size: 2

Duration: 30 minutes

Ingredients:

- 1 tablespoon olive oil
- 1/2 pound cooked corned beef, diced
- 1 large russet potato, diced
- 1/2 medium onion, diced
- 1/2 red bell pepper, diced
- 1/2 teaspoon paprika
- Salt and pepper, to taste
- 2 eggs
- Fresh parsley, chopped (for garnish)

Instructions:

1. **Preheat** your Blackstone griddle over medium-high heat. Ensure the surface is evenly heated to avoid hot spots that could cause uneven cooking.

2. **Spread** the olive oil over the griddle surface. This will help to prevent sticking and ensure your ingredients cook evenly.

3. **Add** the diced potatoes to the griddle first. They take the longest to cook. Spread them out in a single layer for maximum contact with the surface. Cook for about 10 minutes, flipping occasionally, until they start to become golden and crispy.

4. **Incorporate** the diced onion and red bell pepper to the griddle alongside the potatoes. Stir occasionally, allowing them to soften and caramelize, about 5 minutes.

5. **Mix in** the diced corned beef with the potatoes, onions, and bell peppers. Sprinkle the paprika, salt, and pepper over the mixture. Continue to cook, stirring occasionally, for another 5-7 minutes until the corned beef is heated through and the vegetables are tender.

6. **Create** two wells in the hash mixture and crack an egg into each. Cover the eggs with a metal bowl or a lid to trap the heat and cook the eggs to your desired doneness, about 3-4 minutes for a runny yolk.

7. **Garnish** the corned beef hash with fresh parsley before serving directly from the griddle.

8. **Serve** immediately while hot and enjoy a hearty, flavorful breakfast that combines the simplicity of griddle cooking with traditional flavors.

16. Apple Cinnamon Griddle Cakes

🍽 Portion Size: Serves 4

⏳ Duration: 30 minutes

🛒 Ingredients:

- 2 cups all-purpose flour
- 1/4 cup granulated sugar
- 1 tablespoon baking powder
- 1/2 teaspoon salt
- 2 teaspoons ground cinnamon
- 1/4 teaspoon ground nutmeg
- 2 large eggs
- 1 1/2 cups milk
- 1/4 cup unsalted butter, melted
- 1 teaspoon vanilla extract
- 1 cup finely diced apples (peeled)
- Additional butter for griddle
- Maple syrup for serving

Instructions:

1. **Preheat the Blackstone Griddle** over medium heat. A good indicator that your griddle is ready is when a few drops of water flicked onto it dance and evaporate.

2. **Mix Dry Ingredients:** In a large bowl, whisk together the flour, sugar, baking powder, salt, cinnamon, and nutmeg until well combined.

3. **Combine Wet Ingredients:** In a separate bowl, beat the eggs and then mix in the milk, melted butter, and vanilla extract until smooth.

4. **Combine Wet and Dry Mixtures:** Pour the wet ingredients into the dry ingredients. Stir until just combined; it's okay if the batter is a bit lumpy. Gently fold in the diced apples.

5. **Prepare the Griddle:** Lightly butter the griddle surface. This not only prevents sticking but also contributes to a golden crust on the pancakes.

6. **Cook the Griddle Cakes:** Pour 1/4 cup portions of the batter onto the griddle, leaving space between each for spreading. Cook for 2-3 minutes, or until bubbles form on the surface and the edges look set. Flip carefully and cook for another 2-3 minutes on the other side until golden brown and cooked through.

7. **Serve Warm:** Transfer the apple cinnamon griddle cakes to a plate and serve warm with maple syrup. For an extra touch, sprinkle a little more cinnamon on top before serving.

Note: The key to perfect griddle cakes is not to overmix the batter. Overmixing can make the pancakes tough. Also, ensure your griddle is at the right temperature before pouring the batter; too hot, and the outside will burn before the inside is cooked, too cool, and they won't get that nice golden exterior.

17. Grilled Breakfast Pizza

Portion Size: 2

Duration: 25 minutes

Ingredients:

- 1 pre-made pizza crust (12 inches)
- 1/2 cup pizza sauce
- 1 cup shredded mozzarella cheese
- 4 breakfast sausage links, pre-cooked and sliced
- 4 eggs
- 1/2 cup cooked and crumbled bacon
- 1/4 cup diced green bell pepper
- 1/4 cup diced red onion
- Salt and pepper to taste
- 1 tablespoon olive oil
- Fresh basil leaves for garnish (optional)

Instructions:

1. Preheat your Blackstone griddle to medium-high heat, around 375°F to 400°F.

2. Brush the pre-made pizza crust lightly on both sides with olive oil. This helps to create a crispy base.

3. Place the pizza crust on the griddle. Cook for about 2-3 minutes on each side, or until it starts to get crispy and golden brown. Remove and set aside.

4. Lower the griddle heat to medium. In a small bowl, beat the eggs and season with salt and pepper.

5. Pour the beaten eggs onto the griddle and scramble gently. Cook until the eggs are just set, about 2-3 minutes. Remove from the griddle and set aside.

6. Spread the pizza sauce evenly over the crisped pizza crust, leaving a small border around the edges.

7. Sprinkle half of the shredded mozzarella cheese over the sauce.

8. Evenly distribute the scrambled eggs, sliced breakfast sausage, crumbled bacon, diced green bell pepper, and red onion over the cheese.

9. Top with the remaining mozzarella cheese.

10. Carefully place the loaded pizza back onto the griddle. Cover with a griddle dome or aluminum foil to help melt the cheese and warm the toppings, about 5-7 minutes.

11. Once the cheese is melted and bubbly, carefully remove the pizza from the griddle.

12. Garnish with fresh basil leaves if desired. Slice and serve immediately.

18. Sautéed Mushrooms and Spinach Frittata

Portion Size: 2

Duration: 25 minutes

🛒 Ingredients:

- 6 large eggs
- 1/4 cup milk
- 1/2 teaspoon salt
- 1/4 teaspoon black pepper
- 1 tablespoon olive oil
- 1 cup fresh spinach, roughly chopped
- 1 cup mushrooms, sliced
- 1/2 cup shredded cheddar cheese
- 1/4 cup diced onion
- 1 garlic clove, minced

Instructions:

1. **Preheat the Blackstone Griddle** over medium heat. Ensure the surface is evenly heated to avoid hot spots that could cook the frittata unevenly.

2. **Prepare the Egg Mixture**: In a large bowl, whisk together the eggs, milk, salt, and pepper until well combined and slightly frothy. This will help incorporate air into the eggs, making the frittata fluffy.

3. **Sauté the Vegetables**: Add the olive oil to the griddle. Once hot, add the sliced mushrooms and diced onion. Sauté for 3-4 minutes until the mushrooms are golden and the onions are translucent. Add the minced garlic and chopped spinach, cooking for an additional 1-2 minutes until the spinach is wilted. Stir frequently to prevent any garlic from burning.

4. **Combine and Cook**: Spread the sautéed vegetables evenly across the griddle. Pour the egg mixture over the vegetables, ensuring an even distribution. Sprinkle the shredded cheddar cheese on top. Cover with a large basting dome or aluminum foil to trap the heat and allow the frittata to cook through. This should take approximately 6-8 minutes. The covering helps steam the top of the frittata for even cooking.

5. **Check for Doneness**: After 6-8 minutes, lift the cover and check if the frittata is set. The eggs should be firm, and the cheese melted. If it's still runny, cover and cook for an additional 2-3 minutes.

6. **Serve**: Once cooked, carefully slide the frittata onto a cutting board. Let it sit for a minute before slicing into wedges. Serve hot directly from the griddle for the best flavor and texture.

Note: Adjust the heat as needed. If the griddle is too hot, the bottom of the frittata may burn before the top is properly cooked. Conversely, if it's too cool, the frittata won't set properly. Finding the right temperature balance is key to a perfectly cooked frittata.

19. Griddle-Cooked Breakfast Tacos

Portion Size: Serves 2

Duration: 30 minutes

🛒 Ingredients:

- 4 small corn tortillas
- 4 large eggs
- 1/2 cup shredded cheddar cheese

- 1/2 cup cooked black beans, rinsed and drained
- 1 avocado, sliced
- 1/4 cup fresh cilantro, chopped
- 1 small red onion, finely diced
- 1 tomato, diced
- 1 jalapeño, thinly sliced (optional)
- Salt and pepper to taste
- 2 tablespoons olive oil

Instructions:

1. **Preheat the Blackstone Griddle** over medium heat. Ensure it reaches a consistent temperature before adding ingredients.

2. **Prepare the Tortillas**: Brush each corn tortilla lightly with olive oil on both sides. Place them on the hot griddle for about 30 seconds per side or until they are lightly toasted and pliable. Remove and cover with a clean cloth to keep warm.

3. **Cook the Eggs**: Crack the eggs into a bowl and beat them lightly with a fork, seasoning with salt and pepper. Add a tablespoon of olive oil to the griddle. Pour in the eggs and let them sit for a few seconds before scrambling. Cook until they are softly set, stirring occasionally. Remove from the griddle and set aside.

4. **Assemble the Tacos**: On each tortilla, evenly distribute the scrambled eggs. Top with shredded cheddar cheese, allowing the residual heat to melt the cheese slightly.

5. **Add the Toppings**: Spoon over the cooked black beans, followed by slices of avocado, diced tomato, red onion, and jalapeño if using. Sprinkle with fresh cilantro for an added burst of flavor.

6. **Serve Immediately**: Enjoy your Griddle-Cooked Breakfast Tacos hot off the griddle for the best taste. Adjust salt and pepper to your liking.

By following these steps, you'll have delicious, hearty breakfast tacos that are perfect for starting your day. The beauty of cooking on the Blackstone Griddle is the ease with which you can manage multiple ingredients at once, ensuring everything comes together at the right time for the perfect bite.

20. Sweet Potato and Black Bean Hash

Portion Size: 2

Duration: 30 minutes

Ingredients:

- 1 large sweet potato, peeled and diced into 1/2-inch cubes
- 1 can (15 ounces) black beans, rinsed and drained
- 1 red bell pepper, diced
- 1 small red onion, diced
- 2 cloves garlic, minced
- 1 teaspoon ground cumin
- 1/2 teaspoon smoked paprika
- 1/4 teaspoon chili powder
- Salt and pepper to taste

- 2 tablespoons olive oil
- 4 eggs
- Fresh cilantro, for garnish
- Optional: avocado slices and hot sauce for serving

Instructions:

1. Preheat your Blackstone griddle to medium-high heat, around 375°F (190°C).

2. In a large bowl, toss the diced sweet potato with 1 tablespoon of olive oil, salt, and pepper until evenly coated.

3. Spread the sweet potatoes out on the griddle in a single layer. Cook for about 10-12 minutes, stirring occasionally, until they are tender and have a slight char.

4. Push the sweet potatoes to one side of the griddle. Add the remaining tablespoon of olive oil to the empty side of the griddle, then add the red bell pepper and red onion. Cook for about 5 minutes, or until they begin to soften.

5. Add the minced garlic, cumin, smoked paprika, and chili powder to the vegetables. Stir well to combine and cook for an additional 1-2 minutes, or until fragrant.

6. Incorporate the black beans with the vegetable mixture. Cook for another 5 minutes, stirring occasionally, until everything is heated through and well combined. Adjust the seasoning with salt and pepper as needed.

7. Create four wells in the hash mixture and crack an egg into each well. Season the eggs with a little salt and pepper. Cover the eggs with a metal dome or aluminum foil and cook for about 4-5 minutes, or until the eggs are cooked to your desired doneness.

8. Carefully remove the hash and eggs from the griddle and divide between plates. Garnish with fresh cilantro, and if desired, serve with avocado slices and hot sauce on the side.

Enjoy your Sweet Potato and Black Bean Hash, a perfect start to your day with the ease and versatility of your Blackstone Griddle.

21. Griddled Sourdough with Avocado and Poached Egg

Portion Size: 2

Duration: 20 minutes

Ingredients:

- 2 large eggs
- 2 slices of sourdough bread
- 1 ripe avocado
- 1 tablespoon white vinegar
- Salt and pepper to taste
- 2 tablespoons olive oil
- Optional garnish: chili flakes, fresh herbs (e.g., cilantro, parsley), or crumbled feta cheese

Instructions:

1. **Preheat the Blackstone Griddle** to a medium heat, around 375°F (190°C), ensuring it's evenly heated.

2. **Prepare the Poached Eggs:**
   - Fill a medium saucepan with about 3 inches of water and bring to a simmer over medium heat. Add 1 tablespoon of white vinegar to the water.
   - Crack each egg into a small bowl or cup. Gently slide the eggs into the simmering water one at a time. Cook for about 3 to 4 minutes for a soft yolk or adjust the time for your desired doneness.
   - Use a slotted spoon to remove the eggs from the water and set them aside on a plate. Season with a little salt and pepper.

3. **Griddle the Sourdough:**
   - Brush both sides of the sourdough slices with olive oil. Place them on the hot griddle.
   - Cook for about 2 minutes on each side, or until they are golden brown and crispy. Remove and place on serving plates.

4. **Prepare the Avocado:**
   - While the bread is grilling, cut the avocado in half, remove the pit, and scoop the flesh into a bowl. Mash the avocado with a fork until it's creamy but still has some texture. Season with salt and pepper to taste.

5. **Assemble the Dish:**
   - Spread the mashed avocado evenly over the grilled sourdough slices.
   - Carefully place a poached egg on top of each avocado-topped sourdough slice.
   - Optional: Garnish with chili flakes, fresh herbs, or crumbled feta cheese for added flavor and presentation.

6. **Serve Immediately:** Enjoy your Griddled Sourdough with Avocado and Poached Egg while it's warm for the best taste and texture experience.

22. Griddle-Cooked Chorizo and Egg Skillet

Portion Size: 2

Duration: 25 minutes

Ingredients:

- 1/2 lb chorizo sausage, casing removed and crumbled
- 4 large eggs
- 1/4 cup red bell pepper, diced
- 1/4 cup green bell pepper, diced
- 1/4 cup onion, diced
- 1/4 cup shredded cheddar cheese
- 1 tablespoon olive oil
- Salt and pepper, to taste
- Chopped cilantro, for garnish
- 2 tablespoons sour cream, for serving

Instructions:

1. **Preheat the Blackstone griddle** over medium heat. Once hot, add 1 tablespoon of olive oil to the surface.

2. **Cook the chorizo**: Add the crumbled chorizo to the griddle. Use a spatula to break it apart further and stir occasionally. Cook until it's thoroughly browned and crispy, about 5-7 minutes. Transfer the cooked chorizo to a plate and set aside.

3. **Sauté the vegetables**: In the same area of the griddle, add the diced red bell pepper, green bell pepper, and onion. Season with a pinch of salt and pepper. Sauté the vegetables until they are soft and slightly caramelized, about 5 minutes.

4. **Combine chorizo and vegetables**: Return the cooked chorizo to the griddle, mixing it with the sautéed vegetables. Spread the mixture evenly across the griddle to create a flat layer.

5. **Create wells for the eggs**: Make four small wells in the chorizo and vegetable mixture. Crack an egg into each well. Season the eggs with a little salt and pepper.

6. **Cook the eggs**: Allow the eggs to cook within the wells. For sunny-side up, cook until the whites are set but the yolks are still runny, about 3-4 minutes. For over-easy or well-done, flip the eggs carefully and cook to your desired doneness.

7. **Add cheese**: Sprinkle the shredded cheddar cheese over the entire mixture. Let it melt for about 1 minute.

8. **Serve**: Carefully slide a spatula under each egg and a portion of the chorizo and vegetable mixture. Transfer to plates. Garnish with chopped cilantro and a dollop of sour cream on the side.

Enjoy your Griddle-Cooked Chorizo and Egg Skillet, a perfect blend of spicy, savory, and creamy flavors, all cooked to perfection on your Blackstone griddle.

23. Grilled Veggie and Cheese Scramble

Portion Size: 2

Duration: 20 minutes

Ingredients:

- 1 medium zucchini, diced
- 1 red bell pepper, diced
- 1 small red onion, diced
- 6 large eggs
- 1/4 cup milk
- 1/2 cup shredded cheddar cheese
- Salt and pepper to taste
- 2 tablespoons olive oil
- Fresh chives for garnish (optional)

Instructions:

1. **Preheat the Blackstone griddle** over medium heat. Ensure the surface is evenly heated to avoid hot spots that could cause uneven cooking.

2. **Prepare the vegetables**: In a medium bowl, combine the diced zucchini, red bell pepper, and red onion. Drizzle with 1 tablespoon of olive oil and season with salt and pepper. Toss to coat evenly.

3. **Cook the vegetables**: Transfer the vegetable mixture to the preheated griddle. Spread them out into a single layer. Cook for about 5-7 minutes, stirring occasionally, until the vegetables are tender and slightly charred. Once cooked, transfer them to a plate and set aside.

4. **Mix the eggs**: In the same bowl used for the vegetables, whisk together the eggs, milk, salt, and pepper until well combined.

5. **Cook the scrambled eggs**: Add the remaining tablespoon of olive oil to the griddle. Pour in the egg mixture. Allow the eggs to set for a moment before gently stirring with a spatula. Cook for 2-3 minutes, or until the eggs are softly set.

6. **Combine and finish**: Once the eggs are nearly set, add the cooked vegetables back to the griddle. Sprinkle the shredded cheddar cheese over the top. Gently fold everything together until the cheese is melted and the eggs are fully cooked.

7. **Serve**: Divide the scramble between two plates. Garnish with fresh chives if desired. Serve immediately for a warm, comforting, and nutritious breakfast.

24. Buttermilk Pancakes with Fresh Fruit

Portion Size: 4

Duration: 25 minutes

Ingredients:

- 2 cups all-purpose flour
- 2 tablespoons granulated sugar
- 1 tablespoon baking powder
- 1/2 teaspoon salt
- 2 cups buttermilk
- 2 large eggs
- 1/4 cup unsalted butter, melted, plus more for greasing the griddle
- 1 teaspoon vanilla extract
- Fresh fruit (such as sliced strawberries, blueberries, and banana slices) for serving
- Maple syrup, for serving

Instructions:

1. **Preheat the Blackstone Griddle** over medium heat. A temperature of around 350°F (175°C) is ideal for cooking pancakes.

2. **Mix Dry Ingredients:** In a large bowl, whisk together the flour, sugar, baking powder, and salt until well combined.

3. **Combine Wet Ingredients:** In a separate bowl, beat the eggs and then mix in the buttermilk, melted butter, and vanilla extract until smooth.

4. **Combine Wet and Dry Ingredients:** Make a well in the center of the dry ingredients and pour in the wet ingredients. Stir until just combined; it's okay if the batter is a little lumpy. Avoid overmixing to ensure fluffy pancakes.

5. **Grease the Griddle:** Lightly brush the griddle with melted butter. This prevents the pancakes from sticking and adds a slight buttery flavor.

6. **Cook the Pancakes:** Pour 1/4 cup of batter for each pancake onto the griddle. Cook until bubbles form on the surface and the edges look set, about 2 minutes. Flip with a spatula and cook for another 1-2 minutes on the other side until golden brown and cooked through.

7. **Serve with Fresh Fruit:** Transfer the pancakes to a plate and top with fresh fruit of your choice. Drizzle with maple syrup for added sweetness.

8. **Repeat:** Continue with the remaining batter, greasing the griddle as needed. Depending on the size of your griddle, you can cook multiple pancakes at once to serve everyone hot pancakes at the same time.

Note: For the best results, ensure your griddle is evenly heated and properly greased before pouring the batter. Adjust the heat as needed to prevent the pancakes from burning. Enjoy your buttermilk pancakes with the freshness of seasonal fruits and the sweetness of maple syrup, creating a perfect start to your day.

25. Griddled Canadian Bacon and Egg Muffin

Portion Size: 2

Duration: 20 minutes

Ingredients:

- 2 English muffins, split
- 4 slices Canadian bacon
- 2 large eggs
- 2 slices American cheese
- Butter, for griddle
- Salt and pepper, to taste
- Cooking spray (for the griddle)

Instructions:

1. **Preheat the Blackstone Griddle** over medium heat. Ensure it's evenly heated to avoid hot spots that could cause uneven cooking.

2. **Prepare the Muffins:** Lightly butter the cut sides of the English muffins. Place them cut side down on the griddle. Toast for about 1-2 minutes or until golden brown. Remove and set aside.

3. **Cook the Canadian Bacon:** Place the slices of Canadian bacon on the griddle. Cook for about 1 minute per side or until they are slightly browned and warmed through. Transfer them to a plate.

4. **Fry the Eggs:** Spray a small area of the griddle with cooking spray. Crack the eggs onto the griddle and break the yolks slightly with a spatula. Season with salt and pepper. Cook for about 1-2 minutes, then flip carefully. Cook for an additional 1 minute for over-easy eggs, or longer for more well-done eggs.

5. **Assemble the Muffins:** Place a slice of cheese on the bottom half of each toasted English muffin. Top each with two slices of Canadian bacon. Place a fried egg on top of the bacon, then cover with the muffin tops.

6. **Serve Immediately:** The Griddled Canadian Bacon and Egg Muffins are best served hot, allowing the cheese to melt slightly from the warmth of the freshly cooked egg and bacon.

Enjoy a classic breakfast favorite made easy and delicious with your Blackstone Griddle, perfect for a quick, satisfying start to your day.

26. Grilled Breakfast Burrito Bowl

Portion Size: 2

Duration: 30 minutes

Ingredients:

- 4 large eggs
- 1 cup of cooked black beans, rinsed and drained
- 1 cup of cooked quinoa
- 1 avocado, sliced
- 1/2 cup of shredded cheddar cheese
- 1/2 cup of fresh salsa
- 1/4 cup of chopped fresh cilantro
- 1 lime, cut into wedges
- 2 tablespoons of olive oil
- Salt and pepper to taste
- Optional: sliced jalapeños, sour cream

Instructions:

1. **Preheat the Blackstone Griddle** over medium heat. Ensure it reaches a consistent temperature before adding any ingredients. This will help in cooking the eggs evenly.

2. **Prepare the eggs:** In a bowl, whisk the eggs with a pinch of salt and pepper. Heat 1 tablespoon of olive oil on the griddle. Once hot, pour the eggs onto the griddle, stirring gently to scramble. Cook until the eggs are softly set, about 2-3 minutes. Transfer to a plate and set aside.

3. **Warm the black beans and quinoa:** In the same area of the griddle, add the remaining tablespoon of olive oil. Add the black beans and quinoa, spreading them out for even cooking. Stir occasionally, cooking until they are thoroughly warmed, about 5 minutes. Season with salt and pepper to taste.

4. **Assemble the burrito bowls:** Divide the quinoa and black beans evenly between two bowls. Top each with half of the scrambled eggs, shredded cheddar cheese, sliced avocado, and fresh salsa. Garnish with chopped cilantro and a lime wedge.

5. **Optional toppings:** If desired, add sliced jalapeños and a dollop of sour cream to each bowl for extra flavor and heat.

6. **Serve immediately:** Enjoy your Grilled Breakfast Burrito Bowl fresh off the griddle for a hearty and flavorful start to your day. The combination of warm quinoa and beans, soft scrambled eggs, melted cheese, and fresh toppings makes for a satisfying breakfast that's both nutritious and delicious.

27. Griddle-Seared Turkey Sausage Patties

Portion Size: 2

Duration: 25 minutes

🛒 Ingredients:

- 1 lb ground turkey
- 1 teaspoon salt
- 1/2 teaspoon black pepper
- 1/2 teaspoon garlic powder
- 1/2 teaspoon onion powder
- 1/4 teaspoon smoked paprika
- 1/4 teaspoon dried sage
- 1/4 teaspoon dried thyme
- 2 tablespoons olive oil (for griddle)

Instructions:

1. **Prep the Turkey Mixture:** In a large bowl, combine the ground turkey, salt, black pepper, garlic powder, onion powder, smoked paprika, dried sage, and dried thyme. Mix thoroughly until all the spices are well incorporated into the turkey.

2. **Form the Patties:** Divide the turkey mixture into 8 equal portions. Roll each portion into a ball, then flatten into a patty about 1/2 inch thick. This ensures even cooking and a perfect sear.

3. **Preheat the Blackstone Griddle:** Turn your Blackstone griddle to medium-high heat and allow it to preheat for about 5 minutes. A properly preheated griddle is crucial for achieving a good sear on the patties.

4. **Cook the Patties:** Once the griddle is hot, brush it with olive oil to prevent sticking. Place the turkey patties on the griddle, leaving enough space between each one to ensure they cook evenly. Cook for about 5 to 6 minutes on each side, or until the patties are well-browned on the outside and no longer pink in the center. The internal temperature should reach 165°F (74°C) when checked with a meat thermometer.

5. **Rest Before Serving:** Once cooked, transfer the patties to a plate and let them rest for a few minutes. This allows the juices to redistribute throughout the patty, ensuring a moist and flavorful bite.

6. **Serving Suggestions:** Serve these griddle-seared turkey sausage patties alongside your favorite breakfast items such as eggs, pancakes, or wrapped in a breakfast burrito. They're also great for making ahead and reheating for a quick and protein-packed breakfast option during the week.

Remember, the key to perfect griddle-seared turkey sausage patties is not to overcrowd the griddle and to allow the patties to develop a nice crust before flipping. Enjoy your delicious and healthy breakfast!

28. Griddled Peanut Butter and Banana Sandwich

Portion Size: 2

Duration: 15 minutes

🛒 Ingredients:

- 4 slices of whole wheat bread
- 1/4 cup creamy peanut butter
- 1 banana, sliced
- 2 tablespoons unsalted butter, melted
- 1 tablespoon honey (optional)

✼ Instructions:

1. **Preheat the Blackstone Griddle** over medium heat. Ensure it reaches a consistent temperature before starting to cook.

2. **Prepare the Sandwiches**: Spread a generous layer of peanut butter on one side of each slice of bread. Place banana slices over the peanut butter on two of the slices. Drizzle honey over the banana slices if desired for added sweetness. Top with the remaining slices of bread, pressing down gently to secure the fillings.

3. **Griddle the Sandwiches**: Brush both sides of the sandwiches lightly with melted butter. This will help to achieve a golden and crispy exterior.

4. **Cook**: Place the sandwiches on the preheated griddle. Cook for about 2-3 minutes on each side or until the bread is golden brown and crispy, and the peanut butter starts to melt. Use a spatula to press down gently on the sandwiches for even grilling.

5. **Serve**: Once cooked, remove the sandwiches from the griddle and let them sit for a minute before cutting. Slice each sandwich in half and serve warm for a delicious and comforting breakfast.

This recipe combines the rich flavors of peanut butter and banana with the crisp texture of griddled bread, making it a quick and satisfying breakfast option.

29. Griddle-Cooked Oatmeal Pancakes

Portion Size: 2

Duration: 25 minutes

Ingredients:

- 1 cup rolled oats
- 1 cup all-purpose flour
- 2 tablespoons sugar
- 1 tablespoon baking powder
- 1/2 teaspoon salt
- 1 1/2 cups milk
- 1 large egg
- 4 tablespoons unsalted butter, melted, plus more for griddle
- 1 teaspoon vanilla extract
- Optional toppings: fresh berries, maple syrup, powdered sugar

✼ Instructions:

1. **Preheat the Blackstone Griddle** over medium heat. Aim for a surface temperature of around 375°F (190°C), which is ideal for cooking pancakes.

2. **Combine Dry Ingredients**: In a large mixing bowl, whisk together the rolled oats, all-purpose flour, sugar, baking powder, and salt until well mixed.

3. **Mix Wet Ingredients**: In another bowl, beat the egg lightly with a whisk, then add the milk, melted butter, and vanilla extract. Stir until just combined.

4. **Combine Wet and Dry Ingredients**: Pour the wet ingredients into the dry ingredients. Stir gently until just combined. It's crucial not to overmix to ensure your pancakes are fluffy. The batter should be slightly lumpy.

5. **Prepare the Griddle**: Lightly brush the griddle with melted butter. This prevents sticking and adds a subtle buttery flavor to the pancakes.

6. **Cook the Pancakes**: For each pancake, pour about 1/4 cup of batter onto the griddle. Cook for 2-3 minutes, or until bubbles form on the surface and the edges look set. Use a spatula to flip the pancakes carefully and cook for another 1-2 minutes on the other side until golden brown and cooked through.

7. **Serve Immediately**: Transfer the cooked pancakes to plates. If desired, top with fresh berries, a drizzle of maple syrup, and a dusting of powdered sugar for extra sweetness and flavor.

8. **Repeat**: Continue with the remaining batter, adding more butter to the griddle as needed. Depending on the size of your griddle, you can cook multiple pancakes at once to serve everyone hot, fresh pancakes at the same time.

Note: For an added twist, you can stir in a half cup of fresh blueberries or chocolate chips into the batter before cooking.

30. Grilled Zucchini and Egg Whites Omelette

Portion Size: 2

Duration: 20 minutes

Ingredients:
- 1 large zucchini, thinly sliced
- 1 tablespoon olive oil
- Salt and pepper, to taste
- 1 cup egg whites
- 1/4 cup diced red bell pepper
- 1/4 cup diced onion
- 1/2 cup shredded low-fat mozzarella cheese
- 1 tablespoon chopped fresh basil
- Non-stick cooking spray

Instructions:

1. Preheat your Blackstone griddle to medium-high heat. Ensure the surface is clean and ready for cooking.

2. In a bowl, toss the thinly sliced zucchini with olive oil, salt, and pepper until evenly coated.

3. Lay the zucchini slices on the griddle in a single layer. Cook for about 2-3 minutes on each side or until they are tender and have grill marks. Remove the zucchini from the griddle and set aside.

4. Lower the griddle heat to medium. Spray a section of the griddle with non-stick cooking spray.

5. Pour the egg whites onto the griddle, forming a large circle or rectangle, depending on your preference.

6. Sprinkle the diced red bell pepper and onion over the egg whites. Allow to cook for 1-2 minutes until the egg whites start to set on the bottom.

7. Carefully place the grilled zucchini slices on one half of the egg whites. Sprinkle the shredded mozzarella cheese and chopped basil over the zucchini.

8. Using a large spatula, gently fold the other half of the egg whites over the zucchini and cheese. Press down lightly with the spatula to seal the edges.

9. Cook for an additional 2-3 minutes, or until the cheese has melted and the omelette is fully set.

10. Carefully slide the omelette onto a plate. Serve immediately for a warm, nutritious breakfast.

This Grilled Zucchini and Egg Whites Omelette combines the ease of Blackstone griddle cooking with fresh, healthy ingredients for a quick and delicious start to your day.

Chapter 3: 30 Lunch Recipes

31. Griddled Chicken Caesar Wrap

Portion Size: 2

Duration: 20 minutes

Ingredients:

- 2 large chicken breasts, thinly sliced
- Salt and pepper, to taste
- 1 tablespoon olive oil
- 4 large flour tortillas
- 1/2 cup Caesar dressing
- 2 cups romaine lettuce, chopped
- 1/2 cup Parmesan cheese, shaved
- 1/4 cup croutons, lightly crushed

Instructions:

1. **Season the Chicken**: Sprinkle both sides of the chicken breasts with salt and pepper to taste.

2. **Preheat the Blackstone Griddle**: Turn your Blackstone Griddle to medium-high heat and allow it to preheat for about 5 minutes.

3. **Cook the Chicken**: Drizzle olive oil over the hot griddle. Place the chicken slices onto the griddle and cook for about 4-5 minutes on each side, or until fully cooked through and golden brown. Remove the chicken from the griddle and set aside.

4. **Warm the Tortillas**: Lower the griddle heat to medium. Place the flour tortillas on the griddle for about 30 seconds on each side, just until they are warm and pliable. Remove and set aside.

5. **Assemble the Wraps**: Lay out the warmed tortillas on a clean surface. Spread each tortilla with a generous amount of Caesar dressing. Add a layer of chopped romaine lettuce on top of the dressing.

6. **Add Chicken and Toppings**: Slice the cooked chicken into thin strips and divide them evenly among the tortillas, laying them on top of the lettuce. Sprinkle shaved Parmesan cheese and crushed croutons over the chicken.

7. **Roll the Wraps**: Fold in the sides of each tortilla, then roll them up tightly to enclose the filling.

8. **Grill the Wraps**: Place the wraps seam-side down back on the griddle for 1-2 minutes, or until they are crispy and golden brown. Flip carefully and grill the other side for an additional minute.

9. **Serve**: Cut each wrap in half diagonally and serve immediately while hot.

Enjoy your Griddled Chicken Caesar Wrap, a perfect blend of crispy, creamy, and savory flavors, all brought together with the ease of your Blackstone Griddle.

32. Grilled Portobello Mushroom Burger

Portion Size: 2

Duration: 20 minutes

Ingredients:

- 2 large Portobello mushroom caps
- 2 tablespoons olive oil
- Salt and pepper, to taste
- 2 slices of provolone cheese
- 2 hamburger buns
- 1/2 avocado, sliced
- 1 small tomato, sliced
- 1/4 red onion, thinly sliced
- 2 lettuce leaves
- Optional: 1 tablespoon balsamic glaze for drizzling

Instructions:

1. **Preheat the Blackstone Griddle** to medium-high heat, around 375°F (190°C).

2. **Prepare the Mushrooms:** Clean the Portobello mushroom caps with a damp cloth, removing any dirt. Brush both sides of the mushrooms with olive oil and season with salt and pepper.

3. **Grill the Mushrooms:** Place the mushroom caps on the griddle, gill side down first. Cook for about 4 minutes, then flip. Cook for another 4 minutes on the other side.

4. **Add Cheese:** Place a slice of provolone cheese on each mushroom cap during the last minute of cooking to allow the cheese to melt.

5. **Toast the Buns:** Brush the hamburger buns with a little olive oil. Place them on the griddle, cut side down, and toast for about 1 minute or until lightly golden.

6. **Assemble the Burgers:** On the bottom half of each bun, place a lettuce leaf, followed by the grilled Portobello mushroom cap (cheese side up), slices of avocado, tomato, and red onion. If desired, drizzle with balsamic glaze.

7. **Final Touch:** Place the top half of the bun on each burger. Serve immediately for the best taste and texture experience.

Enjoy your Grilled Portobello Mushroom Burger, a hearty and flavorful option for any grilling occasion, perfectly crafted on your Blackstone Griddle.

33. Griddle-Seared Steak Fajitas

Portion Size: 2

Duration: 30 minutes

Ingredients:

- 1 lb flank steak, thinly sliced against the grain
- 2 tablespoons olive oil, divided
- 1 tablespoon lime juice
- 1 teaspoon chili powder
- 1 teaspoon cumin
- 1/2 teaspoon garlic powder
- 1/2 teaspoon onion powder
- Salt and pepper to taste
- 1 large bell pepper, sliced
- 1 large onion, sliced
- 4 flour tortillas
- Optional toppings: sour cream, guacamole, shredded cheese, salsa

Instructions:

1. **Marinate the Steak**: In a bowl, combine 1 tablespoon of olive oil, lime juice, chili powder, cumin, garlic powder, onion powder, salt, and pepper. Add the sliced flank steak to the marinade, ensuring each piece is well-coated. Let it marinate for at least 15 minutes, or up to 1 hour in the refrigerator for more flavor.

2. **Preheat the Griddle**: Turn your Blackstone griddle to medium-high heat and allow it to preheat for about 5 minutes. A properly preheated griddle ensures even cooking and perfect sear marks.

3. **Cook the Vegetables**: Add the remaining tablespoon of olive oil to the griddle. Add the sliced bell pepper and onion, seasoning with a pinch of salt and pepper. Cook for 5-7 minutes, stirring occasionally, until they are soft and slightly charred. Transfer the vegetables to a plate and cover to keep warm.

4. **Griddle the Steak**: Place the marinated steak slices on the griddle in a single layer. Cook for 2-3 minutes on each side, or until they reach your desired level of doneness. Remove the steak from the griddle and let it rest for a few minutes.

5. **Warm the Tortillas**: Reduce the griddle heat to low. Place the flour tortillas on the griddle for about 30 seconds per side, just until they are warm and pliable.

6. **Assemble the Fajitas**: On each warmed tortilla, layer the cooked steak, bell peppers, and onions. Add any optional toppings like sour cream, guacamole, shredded cheese, or salsa as desired.

7. **Serve Immediately**: Roll up the tortillas with the filling inside and serve the fajitas hot. Enjoy the blend of flavors and textures from the perfectly seared steak, soft vegetables, and your choice of toppings, all brought together in a delicious, easy-to-make meal on your Blackstone griddle.

34. Honey Mustard Chicken Skewers

Portion Size: 2

Duration: 30 minutes

Ingredients:

- 1 pound chicken breast, cut into 1-inch cubes
- 1/4 cup honey
- 1/4 cup Dijon mustard
- 1 tablespoon olive oil

- 1 teaspoon garlic powder
- 1/2 teaspoon paprika
- Salt and pepper to taste
- Wooden or metal skewers (if using wooden skewers, soak in water for at least 30 minutes before grilling)

Instructions:

1. **Prepare the Marinade**: In a medium bowl, whisk together honey, Dijon mustard, olive oil, garlic powder, paprika, salt, and pepper until well combined.

2. **Marinate the Chicken**: Add the chicken cubes to the bowl with the marinade. Stir to ensure each piece is evenly coated. Cover the bowl with plastic wrap and refrigerate for at least 15 minutes, or up to 2 hours for more flavor.

3. **Preheat the Blackstone Griddle**: Turn your Blackstone Griddle to medium-high heat, allowing it to preheat for about 5 minutes. A properly preheated griddle ensures the chicken will cook evenly and get a nice sear.

4. **Skewer the Chicken**: Thread the marinated chicken cubes onto the skewers, leaving a small space between each piece to ensure even cooking.

5. **Grill the Skewers**: Lightly oil the griddle surface. Place the chicken skewers on the griddle. Cook for about 4-5 minutes on each side, or until the chicken is fully cooked through and has a nice golden color. The internal temperature should reach 165°F (74°C) when checked with a meat thermometer.

6. **Serve**: Once cooked, remove the chicken skewers from the griddle and let them rest for a couple of minutes. This allows the juices to redistribute, making the chicken more tender and flavorful.

Enjoy your Honey Mustard Chicken Skewers, a simple yet delicious meal that showcases the versatility and ease of cooking with your Blackstone Griddle. Perfect for a quick lunch or a casual outdoor gathering.

35. Grilled Shrimp Tacos with Lime Slaw

Portion Size: 2

Duration: 30 minutes

Ingredients:

- 12 large shrimp, peeled and deveined
- 1 tablespoon olive oil
- 1 teaspoon chili powder
- 1/2 teaspoon ground cumin
- 1/4 teaspoon garlic powder
- Salt and pepper to taste
- 4 small corn tortillas
- 1 cup thinly sliced red cabbage
- 1/4 cup thinly sliced red onion
- 1/4 cup chopped cilantro
- 1 lime, juiced
- 2 tablespoons sour cream
- 1 tablespoon mayonnaise
- 1 teaspoon honey
- 1 avocado, sliced

- Lime wedges for serving

Instructions:

1. **Marinate the Shrimp**: In a bowl, combine shrimp, olive oil, chili powder, ground cumin, garlic powder, salt, and pepper. Toss to coat evenly and set aside to marinate for 10-15 minutes.

2. **Prepare the Lime Slaw**: In another bowl, mix together red cabbage, red onion, cilantro, and lime juice. Season with salt to taste. Set aside.

3. **Mix Sour Cream Sauce**: In a small bowl, whisk together sour cream, mayonnaise, and honey until smooth. Set aside.

4. **Preheat the Blackstone Griddle**: Turn your griddle to medium-high heat and allow it to preheat for about 5 minutes.

5. **Grill the Shrimp**: Place marinated shrimp on the hot griddle. Cook for 2-3 minutes per side or until shrimp are pink and slightly charred. Remove from griddle and keep warm.

6. **Warm the Tortillas**: Reduce the griddle heat to low. Place corn tortillas on the griddle for about 30 seconds per side or until they are warm and pliable. Remove and cover with a cloth to keep warm.

7. **Assemble the Tacos**: Spread a small amount of the sour cream sauce on each tortilla. Add a few slices of avocado, then top with grilled shrimp. Add a generous amount of lime slaw on top of the shrimp.

8. **Serve**: Garnish with additional cilantro if desired and serve with lime wedges on the side.

Enjoy your Grilled Shrimp Tacos with Lime Slaw, a perfect blend of flavors and textures, all brought together on your Blackstone Griddle for a quick and delicious lunch.

36. Griddled Turkey and Avocado Panini

Portion Size: 2

Duration: 20 minutes

Ingredients:

- 4 slices of sourdough or ciabatta bread
- 1/2 lb turkey breast, thinly sliced
- 1 ripe avocado, peeled, pitted, and thinly sliced
- 4 slices of provolone cheese
- 2 tablespoons mayonnaise
- 1 tablespoon Dijon mustard
- 1 tablespoon olive oil
- Salt and pepper to taste
- Optional: 1/2 cup arugula or baby spinach

Instructions:

1. **Preheat the Blackstone Griddle** to medium heat, around 350°F. Ensure it's evenly heated to achieve the perfect sear on your panini.

2. **Prepare the Sandwich Spread**: In a small bowl, mix together the mayonnaise and Dijon mustard. Spread this mixture evenly on one side of each bread slice.

3. **Assemble the Panini**: On two slices of bread (on the side with the spread), layer the thinly sliced turkey, avocado slices, and provolone cheese. If using, add a layer of arugula or baby spinach. Season with a pinch of salt and pepper. Top with the remaining slices of bread, spread side down, to complete the sandwiches.

4. **Grill the Panini**: Brush the outside of each sandwich lightly with olive oil. Place the sandwiches on the hot griddle. Use a heavy skillet or a panini press to press down on the sandwiches gently. Grill for about 3-4 minutes on each side, or until the bread is toasted to a golden brown and the cheese has melted.

5. **Serve**: Once grilled to perfection, remove the panini from the griddle. Let them rest for a minute before cutting each sandwich in half. Serve hot for a delicious and satisfying lunch.

Enjoy your Griddled Turkey and Avocado Panini, a simple yet flavorful meal that showcases the versatility and convenience of cooking with a Blackstone Griddle.

37. Blackstone Grilled Cheese with Tomato Soup

Portion Size: 2

Duration: 30 minutes

Ingredients:

- **For Grilled Cheese:**
  - 4 slices of sourdough bread
  - 4 slices of cheddar cheese
  - 2 tablespoons unsalted butter, at room temperature
- **For Tomato Soup:**
  - 1 tablespoon olive oil
  - 1 small onion, diced
  - 2 cloves garlic, minced
  - 1 can (28 ounces) whole peeled tomatoes, with juice
  - 1 cup chicken or vegetable broth
  - 1 teaspoon sugar
  - Salt and pepper, to taste
  - 1/2 cup heavy cream
  - Fresh basil leaves, for garnish

Instructions:

1. **Preheat the Blackstone Griddle** over medium heat for the grilled cheese and set a saucepan on a stove top for the tomato soup.

2. **Start Tomato Soup:**
   - In the saucepan, heat olive oil over medium heat. Add diced onion and minced garlic, sautéing until the onion is translucent, about 5 minutes.
   - Stir in the whole peeled tomatoes with their juice, chicken or vegetable broth, and sugar. Season with salt and pepper.
   - Bring the mixture to a simmer, breaking up the tomatoes with a spoon. Simmer for 20 minutes, stirring occasionally.

3. **Prepare Grilled Cheese:**
   - Spread butter evenly on one side of each slice of sourdough bread.
   - Place two slices, buttered side down, on the preheated griddle. Top each with two slices of cheddar cheese, then cover with the remaining bread slices, buttered side up.
   - Grill for about 3-4 minutes on each side, or until the bread is golden brown and the cheese has melted. Press down lightly with a spatula for even grilling.

4. **Finish Tomato Soup:**
   - After simmering, remove the soup from heat and let it cool slightly. Puree the soup using an immersion blender until smooth.
   - Stir in the heavy cream and return to low heat, warming through without boiling. Adjust seasoning with salt and pepper as needed.

5. **Serve:**
   - Cut the grilled cheese sandwiches in half diagonally.
   - Ladle the tomato soup into bowls, garnishing with fresh basil leaves.
   - Serve the grilled cheese sandwiches alongside the tomato soup for dipping.

Enjoy a classic comfort meal of Blackstone Grilled Cheese with Tomato Soup, perfect for a quick and satisfying lunch prepared with ease on your Blackstone Griddle.

38. Griddle-Cooked Philly Cheesesteak

Portion Size: 2

Duration: 20 minutes

Ingredients:

- 1/2 lb thinly sliced ribeye steak
- 1 large onion, thinly sliced
- 1 green bell pepper, thinly sliced
- 2 tablespoons olive oil, divided
- Salt and pepper, to taste
- 4 slices provolone cheese
- 2 large hoagie rolls, split
- Optional: mayonnaise, ketchup, or mustard

Instructions:

1. **Preheat the Blackstone Griddle** to medium-high heat, around 375°F (190°C). Ensure the griddle is hot before adding ingredients to achieve a good sear on the meat.

2. **Season the Steak**: Lightly season the ribeye slices with salt and pepper. Set aside.

3. **Cook the Vegetables**: Add 1 tablespoon of olive oil to the griddle. Add the sliced onions and bell peppers. Cook for 5-7 minutes, stirring occasionally, until they are soft and slightly caramelized. Transfer the vegetables to a plate and cover to keep warm.

4. **Cook the Steak**: Add the remaining tablespoon of olive oil to the griddle. Add the seasoned ribeye slices. Cook for about 2 minutes on each side or until the steak reaches your desired level of doneness. Use a spatula to chop the steak into smaller pieces as it cooks.

5. **Combine Steak and Vegetables**: Once the steak is cooked, mix the vegetables back in with the steak on the griddle. Divide the mixture into two portions and top each with two slices of provolone cheese. Allow the cheese to melt over the steak and vegetables, about 1 minute.

6. **Toast the Hoagie Rolls**: Place the hoagie rolls, cut side down, on a cooler part of the griddle. Toast for 1-2 minutes until they are lightly browned and crispy.

7. **Assemble the Sandwiches**: Using a spatula, carefully scoop each portion of the steak and vegetable mixture onto the toasted hoagie rolls. If desired, add mayonnaise, ketchup, or mustard to the rolls before adding the steak mixture.

8. **Serve Immediately**: Enjoy your Griddle-Cooked Philly Cheesesteak hot off the griddle for a classic and satisfying meal.

39. Grilled Veggie and Hummus Wrap

Portion Size: 2

Duration: 20 minutes

Ingredients:

- 2 large whole wheat tortillas
- 1 cup hummus
- 1 zucchini, thinly sliced
- 1 yellow squash, thinly sliced
- 1 red bell pepper, julienned
- 1/2 red onion, thinly sliced
- 1 tablespoon olive oil
- Salt and pepper, to taste
- 1/2 cup baby spinach leaves
- 1/4 cup crumbled feta cheese (optional)

Instructions:

1. **Preheat the Blackstone Griddle** to medium-high heat, around 375°F (190°C). Ensure it's evenly heated for consistent cooking.

2. **Prepare the Vegetables**: In a large bowl, toss the zucchini, yellow squash, red bell pepper, and red onion with olive oil, salt, and pepper until they are evenly coated.

3. **Grill the Vegetables**: Spread the vegetables evenly across the griddle. Cook for about 5-7 minutes, turning occasionally, until they are tender and have nice grill marks. Remove from the griddle and set aside.

4. **Warm the Tortillas**: Place the whole wheat tortillas on the griddle for about 30 seconds to 1 minute per side, just until they are warm and pliable. Remove and set aside.

5. **Assemble the Wraps**: Spread a generous layer of hummus over each tortilla, leaving a small border around the edges. Arrange an even layer of grilled vegetables across the center of each tortilla. Add a handful of baby spinach leaves on top of the vegetables. If using, sprinkle crumbled feta cheese over the spinach.

6. **Roll the Wraps**: Fold in the sides of each tortilla, then roll tightly from the bottom up to enclose the filling. Press gently to seal.

7. **Final Grilling (Optional)**: For a crispy exterior, place the rolled wraps seam-side down on the griddle. Grill for about 2 minutes on each side, or until the wraps are golden brown and slightly crispy.

8. **Serve**: Cut each wrap in half diagonally and serve immediately. Enjoy a delicious and nutritious Grilled Veggie and Hummus Wrap, perfect for a quick and satisfying lunch.

40. Griddle-Seared Tuna Melt

Portion Size: 2

Duration: 20 minutes

Ingredients:
- 2 tuna steaks (about 6 ounces each)
- Salt and pepper, to taste
- 1 tablespoon olive oil
- 4 slices of sourdough bread
- 2 tablespoons mayonnaise
- 1 tablespoon Dijon mustard
- 4 slices of Swiss cheese
- 1/2 red onion, thinly sliced
- 1 tomato, thinly sliced
- 1/4 cup pickles, sliced
- Butter, for griddle

Instructions:

1. **Season the Tuna Steaks:** Sprinkle both sides of the tuna steaks with salt and pepper to taste.

2. **Preheat the Blackstone Griddle:** Turn the griddle to medium-high heat and allow it to preheat for about 5 minutes.

3. **Cook the Tuna:** Brush the griddle with 1 tablespoon of olive oil. Place the tuna steaks on the griddle and cook for about 2-3 minutes per side for medium-rare, or until desired doneness is reached. Remove from the griddle and let them rest for a few minutes before slicing thinly.

4. **Prepare the Bread:** Spread mayonnaise on one side of each slice of sourdough bread. Apply Dijon mustard over the mayonnaise. Arrange slices of Swiss cheese, followed by slices of red onion, tomato, and pickles on two slices of bread.

5. **Assemble the Sandwich:** Add the sliced tuna on top of the vegetables. Top with the remaining slices of bread, mayonnaise side down.

6. **Griddle the Sandwich:** Reduce the griddle heat to medium. Butter the griddle surface. Place the sandwiches on the griddle and cook for about 3-4 minutes on each side, or until the bread is golden brown and the cheese has melted, pressing down gently with a spatula to ensure even cooking.

7. **Serve:** Once cooked, remove the sandwiches from the griddle. Cut in half and serve immediately while hot and melty.

Enjoy your Griddle-Seared Tuna Melt, a gourmet twist on a classic sandwich, perfectly cooked on your Blackstone Griddle.

41. Griddled Chicken Quesadilla

Portion Size: 2

Duration: 20 minutes

Ingredients:
- 2 large flour tortillas
- 1 cup cooked chicken, shredded
- 1 cup shredded Monterey Jack cheese
- 1/2 cup black beans, rinsed and drained
- 1/2 cup corn kernels (fresh, canned, or thawed from frozen)
- 1/4 cup red onion, finely chopped
- 1/4 cup fresh cilantro, chopped
- 1 avocado, sliced
- 1/2 cup salsa
- 2 tablespoons olive oil
- Salt and pepper to taste

Instructions:

1. **Preheat the Blackstone Griddle** to medium-high heat, around 375°F (190°C). This ensures a crisp exterior on the tortillas.

2. **Prepare the Filling**: In a bowl, combine the shredded chicken, black beans, corn, red onion, cilantro, and half of the shredded Monterey Jack cheese. Season with salt and pepper to taste. Mix well to ensure the filling is evenly distributed.

3. **Assemble the Quesadillas**: Lay out the flour tortillas on a clean surface. Divide the chicken mixture evenly among the tortillas, spreading it over one half of each tortilla. Add a few slices of avocado on top of the filling and then sprinkle the remaining cheese over the avocado. Fold the other half of the tortilla over the filling to create a half-moon shape.

4. **Cook the Quesadillas**: Brush the griddle with olive oil to prevent sticking. Place the quesadillas on the griddle and cook for about 3-4 minutes on each side, or until they are golden brown and the cheese has melted. Use a spatula to press down gently on the quesadillas as they cook to ensure even contact with the griddle.

5. **Serve**: Once cooked, transfer the quesadillas to a cutting board. Let them rest for 1-2 minutes before cutting each quesadilla into wedges. Serve with salsa on the side for dipping.

6. **Optional Garnish**: If desired, garnish with additional fresh cilantro or a dollop of sour cream before serving.

By following these steps, you'll enjoy a delicious and satisfying Griddled Chicken Quesadilla, showcasing the versatility and ease of cooking with your Blackstone Griddle. Perfect for a quick lunch or a casual dinner, this recipe brings together the flavors of tender chicken, melted cheese, and fresh vegetables in every bite.

42. Grilled Caprese Sandwich

Portion Size: 2

Duration: 15 minutes

🛒 Ingredients:

- 4 slices of sourdough or ciabatta bread
- 2 large tomatoes, sliced
- 8 ounces fresh mozzarella cheese, sliced
- Fresh basil leaves
- Balsamic glaze
- Salt and pepper, to taste
- 2 tablespoons olive oil

👨‍🍳 Instructions:

1. **Preheat the Blackstone Griddle** to medium heat, around 375°F (190°C). Ensure it's evenly heated for consistent cooking.

2. **Prepare the Sandwiches**: On two slices of bread, layer the sliced tomatoes, fresh mozzarella, and basil leaves. Season with salt and pepper. Drizzle with balsamic glaze. Top with the remaining slices of bread to form sandwiches.

3. **Grill the Sandwiches**: Brush both sides of each sandwich lightly with olive oil. This will help to achieve a golden crust and prevent sticking.

4. **Cook on the Griddle**: Place the sandwiches on the griddle. Cook for about 3-4 minutes on each side, pressing down lightly with a spatula to ensure even contact with the griddle surface. Flip carefully to maintain the sandwich structure. Cook until the bread is toasted to a golden brown and the mozzarella has melted.

5. **Serve Immediately**: Once cooked, remove the sandwiches from the griddle. Cut each sandwich in half and serve hot, allowing the flavors of the melted mozzarella, fresh tomato, and basil to meld beautifully with the crispiness of the bread and the tangy sweetness of the balsamic glaze.

Enjoy your Grilled Caprese Sandwich, a simple yet delicious meal that showcases the ease and versatility of cooking with your Blackstone Griddle.

43. Griddle-Cooked Reuben Sandwich

🍽 Portion Size: 2
⏲ Duration: 20 minutes
🛒 Ingredients:
- 4 slices of rye bread
- 8 oz of corned beef, thinly sliced
- 4 slices of Swiss cheese
- 1 cup of sauerkraut, drained
- 1/4 cup of Thousand Island dressing
- 2 tablespoons butter, softened

👨‍🍳 Instructions:

1. **Preheat the Blackstone Griddle** to medium heat, around 350°F (175°C), ensuring it's evenly heated.

2. **Prepare the Sandwiches**: Spread Thousand Island dressing over one side of each slice of rye bread. On two slices of bread, layer the corned beef, Swiss cheese, and sauerkraut. Top with the remaining slices of bread, dressing side down, to form two sandwiches.

3. **Butter the Bread**: Spread the softened butter on the outside of each sandwich, ensuring both the top and bottom are lightly coated. This helps to achieve a golden, crispy texture.

4. **Griddle the Sandwiches**: Place the sandwiches on the preheated griddle. Cook for about 4-5 minutes on each side, or until the bread is toasted to a golden brown and the cheese has melted. Press down lightly with a spatula for even grilling, but be careful not to squeeze out the fillings.

5. **Check for Doneness**: The sandwiches are ready when they are golden brown on both sides and the cheese is melted. If the cheese isn't melting as quickly as you'd like, you can cover the sandwiches with a metal bowl or a griddle dome to trap the heat and encourage melting.

6. **Serve Hot**: Once cooked, remove the sandwiches from the griddle and let them rest for a minute before cutting. Slice each sandwich in half and serve immediately. Enjoy the melty cheese, warm corned beef, and tangy sauerkraut encased in crispy rye bread.

By following these steps, you'll create a delicious Griddle-Cooked Reuben Sandwich that's perfect for a satisfying lunch. This recipe showcases the versatility and ease of cooking with your Blackstone Griddle, making it a great addition to your outdoor cooking repertoire.

44. Griddled BBQ Pulled Pork Sliders

Portion Size: 2

Duration: 60 minutes

Ingredients:

- 1 lb pulled pork (pre-cooked)
- 1/2 cup BBQ sauce
- 4 slider buns
- 1/4 cup coleslaw
- 2 tablespoons olive oil
- Salt and pepper to taste
- Optional: pickles for garnish

Instructions:

1. **Preheat the Blackstone Griddle**: Turn your griddle to medium heat and allow it to warm up for about 5 minutes. A consistent temperature is key for reheating the pulled pork evenly without drying it out.

2. **Prepare the Pulled Pork**: In a bowl, mix the pre-cooked pulled pork with BBQ sauce until well combined. Season with salt and pepper to taste. Adjust the amount of BBQ sauce based on your preference for a wetter or drier slider filling.

3. **Warm the Pulled Pork**: Spread the olive oil over the griddle surface to prevent sticking. Add the BBQ sauce-coated pulled pork to the griddle. Cook for about 4-5 minutes, stirring occasionally, until the pork is heated through and slightly caramelized on the edges.

4. **Toast the Slider Buns**: Cut the slider buns in half. Place the buns cut side down on a less hot section of the griddle. Toast for 1-2 minutes or until they are lightly golden and crispy. Remove and set aside.

5. **Assemble the Sliders**: Place a generous amount of the warm pulled pork on the bottom half of each slider bun. Top the pork with a tablespoon of coleslaw. If desired, add a couple of pickles for an extra crunch and tanginess.

6. **Serve**: Cap the sliders with the top halves of the buns. Serve immediately while the pulled pork is warm and the buns are still crispy.

Enjoy your Griddled BBQ Pulled Pork Sliders, a quick and delicious lunch prepared on your Blackstone Griddle, perfect for any day of the week.

45. Grilled Mediterranean Chicken Salad

Portion Size: 2
Duration: 30 minutes
Ingredients:
- 2 boneless, skinless chicken breasts
- 1 teaspoon olive oil
- Salt and pepper, to taste
- 1 teaspoon dried oregano
- 4 cups mixed greens (such as arugula, spinach, and romaine)
- 1/2 cup cherry tomatoes, halved
- 1/4 cup sliced cucumber
- 1/4 cup red onion, thinly sliced
- 1/4 cup Kalamata olives, pitted and halved
- 1/4 cup feta cheese, crumbled
- For the dressing:
  - 2 tablespoons olive oil
  - 1 tablespoon balsamic vinegar
  - 1 teaspoon Dijon mustard
  - 1 garlic clove, minced
  - Salt and pepper, to taste

Instructions:

1. **Preheat the Blackstone Griddle** to medium-high heat, around 375°F (190°C).

2. **Prepare the Chicken**: Rub the chicken breasts with 1 teaspoon of olive oil, then season both sides with salt, pepper, and dried oregano.

3. **Grill the Chicken**: Place the chicken on the griddle and cook for about 5-7 minutes per side, or until the internal temperature reaches 165°F (74°C) and the juices run clear. Once cooked, transfer the chicken to a cutting board and let it rest for a few minutes before slicing it thinly.

4. **Prepare the Salad**: In a large bowl, combine the mixed greens, cherry tomatoes, cucumber, red onion, Kalamata olives, and feta cheese. Toss gently to mix.

5. **Make the Dressing**: In a small bowl, whisk together 2 tablespoons of olive oil, balsamic vinegar, Dijon mustard, minced garlic, salt, and pepper until well combined.

6. **Dress the Salad**: Drizzle the dressing over the salad and toss to ensure all the ingredients are evenly coated.

7. **Serve**: Divide the salad between two plates. Top each salad with slices of the grilled chicken. Serve immediately for a fresh and flavorful Mediterranean-inspired meal.

Enjoy your Grilled Mediterranean Chicken Salad, a perfect blend of savory grilled chicken, crisp vegetables, and tangy feta cheese, all brought together with a homemade dressing.

46. Griddle-Seared Beef and Broccoli Stir Fry

Portion Size: 2

Duration: 30 minutes

Ingredients:

- 1 lb beef flank steak, thinly sliced against the grain
- 2 cups broccoli florets
- 2 tablespoons olive oil, divided
- 1 tablespoon garlic, minced
- 1/4 cup soy sauce
- 2 tablespoons brown sugar
- 1 tablespoon oyster sauce
- 1 teaspoon ginger, grated
- 1 tablespoon cornstarch
- 1/4 cup water
- Salt and pepper to taste
- Sesame seeds for garnish (optional)
- Green onions, sliced for garnish (optional)

Instructions:

1. **Prep the Sauce**: In a small bowl, whisk together soy sauce, brown sugar, oyster sauce, and grated ginger until well combined. Set aside.

2. **Mix Cornstarch and Water**: In another small bowl, dissolve cornstarch in water to make a slurry. This will help thicken the sauce later. Set aside.

3. **Preheat the Griddle**: Turn your Blackstone griddle to medium-high heat and allow it to preheat for about 5 minutes. A properly heated griddle ensures a good sear on the beef.

4. **Cook the Beef**: Drizzle 1 tablespoon of olive oil on the griddle. Add the thinly sliced beef in a single layer, seasoning lightly with salt and pepper. Sear for about 2-3 minutes on each side until browned and nearly cooked through. Remove beef from the griddle and set aside.

5. **Sauté Vegetables**: Add the remaining tablespoon of olive oil to the griddle. Toss in the broccoli florets and minced garlic, stirring frequently. Cook for about 4-5 minutes until the broccoli is vibrant and tender-crisp.

6. **Combine Beef and Broccoli**: Return the beef to the griddle with the broccoli. Stir in the prepared sauce, ensuring the beef and broccoli are well coated.

7. **Thicken the Sauce**: Pour the cornstarch slurry over the beef and broccoli, stirring constantly. The sauce will begin to thicken almost immediately. Cook for an additional 2-3 minutes, allowing the sauce to bubble and thicken to coat the ingredients.

8. **Garnish and Serve**: Sprinkle sesame seeds and sliced green onions over the top for garnish, if desired. Serve hot directly from the griddle.

Enjoy a flavorful and satisfying Griddle-Seared Beef and Broccoli Stir Fry, showcasing the versatility and ease of cooking with your Blackstone griddle. Perfect for a quick and delicious lunch that's sure to impress.

47. Griddled Teriyaki Chicken Bowl

Portion Size: 2

Duration: 30 minutes

Ingredients:

- 2 boneless, skinless chicken breasts
- 1/2 cup teriyaki sauce, plus extra for serving
- 1 cup cooked white rice
- 1 cup broccoli florets
- 1 red bell pepper, sliced
- 1 tablespoon olive oil
- Salt and pepper to taste
- Sesame seeds, for garnish
- Sliced green onions, for garnish

Instructions:

1. **Marinate the Chicken**: Place the chicken breasts in a shallow dish and pour 1/2 cup of teriyaki sauce over them. Ensure both sides are coated. Cover and refrigerate for at least 15 minutes, or up to 1 hour for deeper flavor.

2. **Preheat the Blackstone Griddle**: Turn your Blackstone Griddle to medium-high heat, allowing it to warm up for about 5 minutes.

3. **Grill the Chicken**: Remove the chicken from the marinade, discarding any excess sauce. Place the chicken on the griddle and cook for 5-7 minutes on each side, or until the internal temperature reaches 165°F (74°C). Once cooked, transfer the chicken to a cutting board and let it rest for a few minutes before slicing it into strips.

4. **Cook the Vegetables**: While the chicken is resting, add the broccoli florets and red bell pepper slices to the griddle. Drizzle with olive oil and season with salt and pepper. Grill the vegetables for about 5-7 minutes, stirring occasionally, until they are tender and have some charred edges.

5. **Assemble the Bowls**: Divide the cooked white rice between two bowls. Top each bowl with sliced chicken, grilled broccoli, and red bell pepper. Drizzle additional teriyaki sauce over the top if desired.

6. **Garnish and Serve**: Sprinkle sesame seeds and sliced green onions over each bowl for garnish. Serve immediately, offering a delicious blend of savory teriyaki chicken, fluffy rice, and grilled vegetables, all prepared effortlessly on your Blackstone Griddle.

48. Grilled Fish Tacos with Mango Salsa

Portion Size: 2

Duration: 30 minutes

Ingredients:

- 2 tilapia fillets (or any white fish of your choice)
- 1 tablespoon olive oil
- 1 teaspoon chili powder

- 1 teaspoon cumin
- Salt and pepper to taste
- 4 small corn tortillas
- 1 ripe mango, diced
- 1/4 red onion, finely chopped
- 1/4 cup fresh cilantro, chopped
- Juice of 1 lime
- 1 avocado, sliced
- 1/4 cup shredded cabbage

Instructions:

1. **Preheat the Blackstone Griddle** over medium-high heat. A consistent temperature is key for perfectly grilled fish.

2. **Season the Fish**: In a small bowl, mix together the olive oil, chili powder, cumin, salt, and pepper. Brush this mixture on both sides of the tilapia fillets, ensuring they are well coated.

3. **Grill the Fish**: Place the seasoned tilapia fillets on the hot griddle. Cook for about 3-4 minutes on each side, or until the fish is opaque and flakes easily with a fork. Once cooked, transfer the fish to a plate and gently break into smaller pieces with a fork.

4. **Warm the Tortillas**: Lower the griddle heat to medium. Place the corn tortillas on the griddle for about 30 seconds to 1 minute per side, or until they are warm and slightly charred. Keep them wrapped in a clean cloth to stay warm.

5. **Make the Mango Salsa**: In a medium bowl, combine the diced mango, red onion, cilantro, and lime juice. Stir well to mix. Season with salt to taste.

6. **Assemble the Tacos**: On each warmed tortilla, lay a portion of the grilled fish. Top with mango salsa, a few slices of avocado, and a sprinkle of shredded cabbage.

7. **Serve Immediately**: Enjoy your Grilled Fish Tacos with Mango Salsa fresh off the griddle. The combination of spicy fish, sweet mango salsa, and creamy avocado creates a delicious and satisfying meal perfect for any lunch occasion.

By following these steps, you'll have a delightful meal that showcases the versatility and ease of cooking with your Blackstone Griddle.

49. Griddle-Cooked Buffalo Chicken Wrap

Portion Size: 2

Duration: 20 minutes

Ingredients:

- 2 large chicken breasts
- 1/2 cup buffalo sauce
- 2 tablespoons ranch dressing
- 1/4 cup crumbled blue cheese
- 1/2 cup shredded lettuce

- 2 large flour tortillas
- 1 tablespoon olive oil
- Salt and pepper, to taste
- Optional: sliced tomatoes, diced celery

Instructions:

1. **Preheat the Blackstone Griddle** over medium-high heat. Ensure it's evenly heated to achieve the perfect sear on the chicken.

2. **Prepare the Chicken**: Season the chicken breasts with salt and pepper. Lightly brush them with olive oil to prevent sticking and enhance flavor.

3. **Cook the Chicken**: Place the chicken breasts on the griddle. Cook for about 5-7 minutes on each side, or until the internal temperature reaches 165°F (74°C) and they're nicely charred on the outside. Once cooked, transfer the chicken to a cutting board.

4. **Shred the Chicken**: Using two forks, shred the cooked chicken into bite-sized pieces. In a bowl, toss the shredded chicken with buffalo sauce until evenly coated.

5. **Warm the Tortillas**: Place the flour tortillas on the griddle for about 30 seconds to 1 minute on each side, just until they are warm and pliable.

6. **Assemble the Wraps**: Lay out the warmed tortillas on a flat surface. Spread a tablespoon of ranch dressing over each tortilla. Divide the buffalo chicken evenly between the tortillas, placing it in the center. Top with crumbled blue cheese and shredded lettuce. Add sliced tomatoes and diced celery if desired.

7. **Roll the Wraps**: Fold in the sides of each tortilla, then roll tightly to enclose the filling. For a crispy exterior, place the wraps seam-side down on the griddle for 1-2 minutes, or until golden and crisp.

8. **Serve**: Cut the wraps in half, if desired, and serve immediately. Enjoy the spicy, tangy flavors of these Griddle-Cooked Buffalo Chicken Wraps, perfect for a quick and satisfying lunch.

50. Grilled Italian Sausage and Peppers

Portion Size: 2

Duration: 30 minutes

Ingredients:

- 4 Italian sausages (about 1 lb)
- 2 bell peppers (preferably one red and one green), sliced into strips
- 1 large onion, sliced into strips
- 2 tablespoons olive oil
- Salt and pepper, to taste
- Optional: crushed red pepper flakes for added heat
- 4 hoagie rolls, split

Instructions:

1. **Preheat the Blackstone Griddle** over medium-high heat. A consistent temperature is crucial for grilling sausages evenly without burning them.

2. **Prepare the Vegetables**: In a large bowl, toss the sliced bell peppers and onion with olive oil, salt, and pepper until they are evenly coated. If you like your sausage and peppers with a bit of a kick, sprinkle some crushed red pepper flakes into the mix.

3. **Grill the Sausages**: Place the Italian sausages on the hot griddle. Grill them for about 5-7 minutes per side, turning occasionally, until they are browned on all sides and cooked through. The internal temperature should reach 160°F when measured with a meat thermometer. Once cooked, transfer the sausages to a plate and tent with foil to keep warm.

4. **Cook the Vegetables**: In the same griddle, add the seasoned bell peppers and onion. Grill the vegetables, stirring occasionally, for about 10-12 minutes, or until they are soft and slightly charred. This will give them a sweet, roasted flavor that complements the sausages beautifully.

5. **Warm the Hoagie Rolls**: Reduce the griddle heat to low. Open the hoagie rolls and place them cut side down on the griddle. Warm them for about 1-2 minutes, or just until they are lightly toasted. This step adds a nice crunch and warmth to your sandwich.

6. **Assemble the Sandwiches**: Slice the grilled sausages lengthwise, being careful not to cut all the way through. Place a sausage on each hoagie roll and top generously with the grilled peppers and onions.

7. **Serve Immediately**: Enjoy your Grilled Italian Sausage and Peppers sandwiches hot off the griddle. Serve them with a side of your choice or enjoy them as is for a satisfying and flavorful lunch.

51. Griddled Ham and Swiss on Rye

Portion Size: 2

Duration: 20 minutes

Ingredients:
- 4 slices of rye bread
- 4 slices of ham, about 1/4 inch thick
- 4 slices of Swiss cheese
- 2 tablespoons Dijon mustard
- 2 tablespoons mayonnaise
- 1 tablespoon unsalted butter, for griddling
- Optional: Pickle slices for serving

Instructions:

1. **Preheat the Blackstone Griddle** to medium heat, aiming for a surface temperature of around 350°F (175°C).

2. **Prepare the Sandwich Spread**: In a small bowl, mix together the Dijon mustard and mayonnaise until well combined. Spread this mixture evenly on one side of each slice of rye bread.

3. **Assemble the Sandwiches**: On two of the slices of rye bread (on the side with the spread), layer each with two slices of ham and two slices of Swiss cheese. Top with the remaining slices of bread, spread side down, to form two sandwiches.

4. **Griddle the Sandwiches**: Melt the butter on the griddle, spreading it evenly over the cooking surface. Place the assembled sandwiches on the griddle. Cook for about 3-4 minutes on each side, or until the bread is toasted to a golden brown and the cheese has melted. Use a spatula to press down gently on the sandwiches for even grilling.

5. **Serving**: Once cooked, transfer the sandwiches to a cutting board. If desired, cut each sandwich in half diagonally. Serve immediately, optionally with pickle slices on the side.

Enjoy your Griddled Ham and Swiss on Rye, a classic sandwich with a delicious twist, perfectly cooked on your Blackstone Griddle for a quick and satisfying lunch.

52. Griddle-Seared Veggie Burger

Portion Size: 2

Duration: 20 minutes

Ingredients:
- 2 veggie burger patties (store-bought or homemade)
- 2 whole wheat hamburger buns
- 1 tablespoon olive oil
- 1/4 cup mayonnaise
- 1 tablespoon barbecue sauce
- 1 avocado, sliced
- 1 tomato, sliced
- 1/2 red onion, thinly sliced
- 1 cup mixed greens (spinach, arugula, etc.)
- Salt and pepper to taste

Instructions:

1. **Preheat the Blackstone Griddle** over medium heat. Aim for a surface temperature of around 350°F (175°C). This ensures a good sear without burning the patties.

2. **Prepare the Sauce**: In a small bowl, mix together the mayonnaise and barbecue sauce. Set aside. This will be used to spread on the buns for added flavor.

3. **Grill the Veggie Burgers**: Brush the veggie patties lightly with olive oil on both sides. Season with salt and pepper. Place the patties on the griddle and cook for about 4 minutes on each side or until they are heated through and have nice grill marks.

4. **Toast the Buns**: Split the whole wheat hamburger buns and place them cut side down on the griddle. Toast for 1-2 minutes or until they are lightly golden. Remove and set aside.

5. **Assemble the Burgers**: Spread a generous amount of the mayonnaise-barbecue sauce mixture on the bottom half of each bun. Place a veggie burger on each bun, followed by slices of avocado, tomato, and red onion. Add a handful of mixed greens on top.

6. **Final Touch**: Place the top half of the bun on each burger. Press down gently to secure the toppings.

7. **Serve Immediately**: Enjoy your Griddle-Seared Veggie Burger hot off the griddle. The combination of the savory veggie patty with the creamy sauce, fresh vegetables, and toasted bun makes for a delicious and satisfying meal.

53. Grilled Margherita Flatbread

Portion Size: 2

Duration: 20 minutes

Ingredients:
- 1 large flatbread or naan bread
- 1/2 cup pizza sauce
- 1 cup shredded mozzarella cheese
- 1 large tomato, thinly sliced
- 1/4 cup fresh basil leaves, torn
- 2 tablespoons olive oil
- Salt and pepper, to taste
- Balsamic glaze, for drizzling (optional)

Instructions:

1. **Preheat the Blackstone Griddle** to medium-high heat, aiming for a surface temperature of around 400°F (204°C). This ensures a crispy base and perfectly melted cheese.

2. **Prepare the Flatbread**: Brush one side of the flatbread lightly with olive oil. This will help to create a crispy texture when grilled.

3. **Grill the Flatbread**: Place the flatbread, oiled side down, on the hot griddle. Grill for about 2 minutes or until it is lightly crispy and has grill marks. Watch closely to avoid burning.

4. **Add Toppings**: Spread the pizza sauce evenly over the grilled side of the flatbread, leaving a small border around the edges. Sprinkle the shredded mozzarella cheese over the sauce, then arrange the tomato slices on top. Season with salt and pepper to taste.

5. **Grill the Margherita Flatbread**: Lower the griddle heat to medium. Carefully slide the flatbread back onto the griddle and cover with a basting dome or aluminum foil. Cook for 5-7 minutes, or until the cheese is melted and bubbly. If you don't have a cover, you can skip this step; the cheese will still melt from the residual heat.

6. **Add Fresh Basil**: Once the cheese is melted, remove the flatbread from the griddle and immediately sprinkle with fresh basil leaves. The heat from the flatbread will gently wilt the basil, releasing its aroma.

7. **Serve**: Drizzle with balsamic glaze if desired for an added depth of flavor. Slice the Grilled Margherita Flatbread into pieces and serve hot.

This Grilled Margherita Flatbread recipe showcases the simplicity and deliciousness of Blackstone griddle cooking, making it a perfect quick and flavorful lunch option.

54. Griddled Chicken Pesto Panini

Portion Size: 2

Duration: 20 minutes

Ingredients:
- 2 chicken breasts, thinly sliced
- 4 slices of sourdough or ciabatta bread
- 4 tablespoons pesto sauce

- 1 tomato, sliced
- 4 slices mozzarella cheese
- Salt and pepper, to taste
- 2 tablespoons olive oil

🍴 Instructions:

1. **Preheat the Blackstone Griddle** to medium-high heat, around 375°F (190°C).

2. **Season the Chicken**: Lightly season the chicken breast slices with salt and pepper on both sides.

3. **Cook the Chicken**: Drizzle 1 tablespoon of olive oil onto the griddle. Place the chicken slices on the griddle and cook for about 3-4 minutes per side, or until fully cooked and golden brown. Remove the chicken from the griddle and set aside.

4. **Assemble the Paninis**: Spread 1 tablespoon of pesto sauce on one side of each bread slice. On two slices of bread, layer the cooked chicken, tomato slices, and mozzarella cheese. Top with the remaining slices of bread, pesto side down.

5. **Grill the Paninis**: Drizzle the remaining olive oil over the griddle. Place the assembled paninis on the griddle. Press down gently with a spatula or a panini press if available. Grill for about 3-5 minutes per side, or until the bread is toasted and crispy and the cheese has melted.

6. **Serve**: Cut each panini in half and serve hot. Enjoy your Griddled Chicken Pesto Panini with a side of your choice for a delicious and satisfying lunch.

55. *Grilled Cuban Sandwich*

🍽 Portion Size: 2

⏳ Duration: 30 minutes

🛒 Ingredients:
- 4 slices of Cuban bread (or a hearty, crusty bread like French or Italian if Cuban is unavailable)
- 8 slices of deli ham
- 1 lb roasted pork, thinly sliced
- 8 slices of Swiss cheese
- Dill pickles, sliced
- Yellow mustard
- 2 tablespoons unsalted butter, at room temperature

🍴 Instructions:

1. **Preheat the Blackstone Griddle** to medium-high heat, around 350°F to 375°F. A properly preheated griddle ensures even cooking and perfect grill marks.

2. **Prepare the Sandwiches**: Spread a generous amount of yellow mustard on the inside of each slice of bread. On the bottom slices, layer the ham, roasted pork, Swiss cheese, and dill pickles evenly. Place the top slices of bread over the pickles to complete the sandwiches.

3. **Butter and Grill**: Spread the outside of each sandwich with a thin layer of butter. This will help to achieve a golden, crispy exterior.

4. **Cook the Sandwiches**: Place the sandwiches on the hot griddle. Use a heavy skillet or a griddle press to press down on the sandwiches gently. This helps to compact the sandwich and ensures even contact with the griddle surface, creating those characteristic grill marks.

5. **Flip and Press**: After about 3-4 minutes, or once the bottom bread slice is golden brown and crispy, carefully flip the sandwiches. Press down again with the skillet or press and cook for another 3-4 minutes, or until the second side is also golden brown and the cheese has melted.

6. **Serve**: Once cooked, remove the sandwiches from the griddle. Let them rest for a minute before slicing each sandwich in half diagonally.

Enjoy your Grilled Cuban Sandwich with a side of plantain chips or a light salad for a complete and satisfying meal.

56. Griddle-Cooked Asian Lettuce Wraps

Portion Size: 2

Duration: 20 minutes

Ingredients:

- 1 lb ground chicken
- 1 tablespoon soy sauce
- 1 tablespoon hoisin sauce
- 1 teaspoon sesame oil
- 1/2 teaspoon ground ginger
- 1 clove garlic, minced
- 1/4 cup green onions, chopped
- 1/4 cup water chestnuts, finely diced
- Salt and pepper, to taste
- 8-10 large lettuce leaves (such as Bibb or butter lettuce)
- Optional garnishes: additional chopped green onions, sesame seeds, sriracha sauce

Instructions:

1. **Preheat the Blackstone Griddle** over medium-high heat. A consistent temperature is crucial for cooking the ground chicken evenly.

2. **Season the Chicken**: In a large bowl, combine the ground chicken with soy sauce, hoisin sauce, sesame oil, ground ginger, minced garlic, and a pinch of salt and pepper. Mix well to ensure the chicken is evenly seasoned.

3. **Cook the Chicken**: Lightly oil the griddle surface with a bit of sesame oil to prevent sticking. Add the seasoned ground chicken to the griddle. Use a spatula to break it apart into smaller pieces. Cook for about 5-7 minutes, or until the chicken is fully cooked through and slightly crispy on the outside.

4. **Add Vegetables**: Once the chicken is nearly cooked, stir in the chopped green onions and diced water chestnuts. Cook for an additional 2-3 minutes, allowing the flavors to meld together and the water chestnuts to soften slightly.

5. **Prepare the Lettuce**: While the chicken cooks, rinse and dry the lettuce leaves. Arrange them on a serving platter. The lettuce will serve as the cups for the chicken mixture.

6. **Assemble the Lettuce Wraps**: Spoon a generous amount of the cooked chicken mixture into the center of each lettuce leaf. If desired, garnish with additional chopped green onions, sesame seeds, and a drizzle of sriracha sauce for extra heat.

7. **Serve Immediately**: Enjoy the Griddle-Cooked Asian Lettuce Wraps while the filling is warm. The crispness of the lettuce combined with the savory, flavorful chicken creates a delightful contrast in textures and flavors.

By following these detailed steps, you'll enjoy a quick, healthy, and delicious meal that showcases the versatility and ease of cooking with your Blackstone Griddle.

57. Griddled Lobster Roll

Portion Size: 2

Duration: 30 minutes

Ingredients:

- 2 fresh lobster tails (about 4-6 ounces each)
- 2 tablespoons unsalted butter, melted
- 1/2 teaspoon garlic powder
- 1/2 teaspoon paprika
- Salt and black pepper, to taste
- 2 tablespoons mayonnaise
- 1 tablespoon lemon juice
- 1/2 celery stalk, finely diced
- 2 tablespoons fresh chives, chopped
- 2 New England-style hot dog buns
- Additional unsalted butter, for toasting buns
- Lemon wedges, for serving

Instructions:

1. **Prepare the Lobster:** Preheat your Blackstone griddle to medium-high heat, around 400°F. Butterfly the lobster tails by cutting through the top shell lengthwise with kitchen shears, then press the shell open. Remove the meat, and chop it into bite-sized pieces.

2. **Season and Cook Lobster:** In a bowl, mix the chopped lobster meat with melted butter, garlic powder, paprika, salt, and black pepper. Spread the lobster evenly on the hot griddle. Cook for about 4-5 minutes, stirring occasionally, until the lobster is fully cooked and slightly charred. Remove from the griddle and set aside.

3. **Mix Lobster Salad:** In a mixing bowl, combine the cooked lobster, mayonnaise, lemon juice, diced celery, and chives. Stir gently until well mixed. Taste and adjust seasoning with salt and pepper as needed.

4. **Toast the Buns:** Butter the outside of each hot dog bun. Place the buns on the griddle, turning once, until both sides are golden brown, about 1-2 minutes per side.

5. **Assemble the Lobster Rolls:** Spoon the lobster salad mixture generously into each toasted bun.

6. **Serve:** Serve the lobster rolls immediately with lemon wedges on the side for squeezing over the top. Enjoy a taste of New England right from your Blackstone griddle.

This Griddled Lobster Roll recipe brings the quintessential New England summer sandwich to your backyard, combining the luxury of lobster with the practicality and fun of griddle cooking.

58. Grilled Chicken Gyros with Tzatziki

Portion Size: 2

Duration: 30 minutes

Ingredients:

- 1 lb chicken breast, thinly sliced
- 1 tablespoon olive oil
- 1 teaspoon garlic powder
- 1 teaspoon oregano
- Salt and pepper, to taste
- 4 pita breads
- 1/2 cup tzatziki sauce
- 1 tomato, sliced
- 1/2 red onion, thinly sliced
- 1/4 cup crumbled feta cheese
- 1/4 cup chopped lettuce

Instructions:

1. **Preheat the Blackstone Griddle** to medium-high heat. Ensure it's evenly heated to achieve the perfect sear on the chicken.

2. **Season the Chicken**: In a mixing bowl, combine the thinly sliced chicken breast with olive oil, garlic powder, oregano, salt, and pepper. Toss until the chicken is well coated with the seasoning.

3. **Cook the Chicken**: Place the seasoned chicken slices onto the hot griddle. Cook for about 3-4 minutes on each side, or until the chicken is fully cooked and has a nice golden-brown exterior. Remove the chicken from the griddle and set aside, keeping it warm.

4. **Warm the Pita Breads**: Lower the griddle heat to medium. Place the pita breads on the griddle for about 1 minute on each side, just until they are warm and slightly toasted. Remove and set aside.

5. **Assemble the Gyros**: On each pita bread, spread a generous amount of tzatziki sauce. Add a portion of the cooked chicken, followed by slices of tomato, red onion, crumbled feta cheese, and chopped lettuce.

6. **Fold and Serve**: Carefully fold the pita bread over the filling. If desired, wrap the bottom half of the gyro in aluminum foil or parchment paper for easier handling.

Enjoy your Grilled Chicken Gyros with Tzatziki, a delicious and easy-to-make lunch that brings the flavors of Mediterranean cuisine right to your Blackstone Griddle.

59. Griddle-Seared Eggplant Parmesan

Portion Size: 2

⏳ Duration: 30 minutes

🛒 Ingredients:
- 1 large eggplant, sliced into 1/2-inch rounds
- 2 cups marinara sauce
- 1 cup shredded mozzarella cheese
- 1/2 cup grated Parmesan cheese
- 1/4 cup fresh basil leaves, chopped
- 2 tablespoons olive oil
- Salt and pepper, to taste
- 1 teaspoon garlic powder
- 1 teaspoon Italian seasoning

👨‍🍳 Instructions:

1. **Preheat the Blackstone Griddle** to medium-high heat, around 375°F (190°C).

2. **Prepare the Eggplant**: Season both sides of the eggplant slices with salt, pepper, garlic powder, and Italian seasoning.

3. **Griddle the Eggplant**: Brush the griddle with olive oil and place the seasoned eggplant slices on it. Cook for about 4-5 minutes on each side, or until they are tender and have nice grill marks. Remove the eggplant slices from the griddle and set aside.

4. **Assemble the Eggplant Parmesan**: On the griddle, lower the heat to medium. Start by spreading a thin layer of marinara sauce directly on the griddle surface. Place the grilled eggplant slices over the sauce. Spoon more marinara sauce over each slice, then sprinkle with mozzarella and Parmesan cheeses.

5. **Melt the Cheese**: Cover the eggplant slices with a griddle dome or a large metal bowl to trap the heat and melt the cheese. This should take about 3-5 minutes. Be careful not to let the bottom burn by adjusting the heat as necessary.

6. **Garnish and Serve**: Once the cheese is melted and bubbly, carefully remove the eggplant Parmesan from the griddle with a spatula. Garnish with chopped fresh basil before serving.

Enjoy your Griddle-Seared Eggplant Parmesan, a delicious and straightforward dish that brings the classic flavors of Italy to your outdoor cooking experience.

60. Grilled Sweet Chili Tofu Sandwich

🍽 Portion Size: 2

⏳ Duration: 20 minutes

🛒 Ingredients:
- 1 block (14 oz) firm tofu, pressed and sliced into 1/2-inch thick slabs
- 1/4 cup sweet chili sauce, plus extra for serving
- 2 tablespoons soy sauce
- 1 tablespoon olive oil
- 1 teaspoon garlic powder
- 1/2 teaspoon ginger powder
- 4 slices of whole grain bread

- 1 avocado, sliced
- 1/4 cup shredded carrots
- 1/4 cup sliced cucumber
- 1/4 cup fresh cilantro leaves
- Salt and pepper to taste

Instructions:

1. **Marinate the Tofu**: In a shallow dish, whisk together the sweet chili sauce, soy sauce, garlic powder, and ginger powder. Add the tofu slices, ensuring each piece is well-coated with the marinade. Let it sit for at least 10 minutes, flipping halfway through for even marination.

2. **Preheat the Griddle**: Turn your Blackstone griddle to medium-high heat. Allow it to preheat for about 5 minutes, ensuring an even cooking surface.

3. **Grill the Tofu**: Brush the griddle lightly with olive oil. Place the marinated tofu slices on the griddle, seasoning them with a pinch of salt and pepper. Grill for about 3-4 minutes on each side, or until they are golden brown and slightly charred around the edges. Remove and set aside.

4. **Toast the Bread**: Lower the griddle heat to medium. Place the slices of bread directly on the griddle, toasting for about 1-2 minutes on each side, or until they are lightly crispy and golden. Remove and set aside.

5. **Assemble the Sandwiches**: Spread a thin layer of sweet chili sauce on one side of each bread slice. On two slices of bread, layer the grilled tofu, followed by avocado slices, shredded carrots, cucumber slices, and fresh cilantro.

6. **Top and Serve**: Place the remaining slices of bread on top, sauce-side down, to complete the sandwiches. Serve immediately, cutting each sandwich in half if desired.

Enjoy your Grilled Sweet Chili Tofu Sandwich, a flavorful and satisfying meal that brings the best out of your Blackstone griddle with minimal effort and maximum taste.

BONUS

By scanning the QR Code below you can download over 3 hours of video recipes in collaboration with "Cooking with Kirby" and your FREE eBook "Exclusive Argentine Asado recipes and delicious Turkish dishes"

Please note the download file is about 10 Gb.

Chapter 4: 30 Dinner Recipes

61. Griddled Lemon Herb Chicken

Portion Size: 2

Duration: 25 minutes

Ingredients:
- 2 boneless, skinless chicken breasts
- 2 tablespoons olive oil
- 1 lemon, zested and juiced
- 2 cloves garlic, minced
- 1 tablespoon fresh rosemary, chopped
- 1 tablespoon fresh thyme, chopped
- Salt and pepper, to taste
- Additional lemon wedges, for serving

Instructions:
1. **Prep the Chicken**: Place chicken breasts between two pieces of plastic wrap and gently pound with a meat mallet or rolling pin to an even thickness of about 1/2 inch. This ensures even cooking.

2. **Marinate**: In a small bowl, combine olive oil, lemon zest, lemon juice, minced garlic, rosemary, thyme, salt, and pepper. Whisk to blend. Pour the marinade over the chicken in a shallow dish, ensuring both sides are well-coated. Let marinate for at least 15 minutes at room temperature, or up to 1 hour in the refrigerator for deeper flavor.

3. **Preheat the Griddle**: Heat your Blackstone griddle over medium-high heat. A drop of water should sizzle on contact when it's ready.

4. **Grill the Chicken**: Remove the chicken from the marinade, letting excess drip off. Place the chicken breasts on the hot griddle. Cook for about 5-7 minutes on each side, or until the chicken is golden brown on the outside and reaches an internal temperature of 165°F. Avoid moving the chicken around too much as it cooks to get a nice sear.

5. **Rest**: Transfer the cooked chicken to a plate and let it rest for a few minutes. This helps retain the juices, making the chicken more tender.

6. **Serve**: Slice the chicken against the grain into strips. Serve hot, garnished with additional lemon wedges on the side for extra flavor.

Enjoy your Griddled Lemon Herb Chicken, a flavorful and simple dish that highlights the ease and versatility of cooking with your Blackstone Griddle. Perfect for a quick yet delicious dinner.

62. Grilled Garlic Butter Shrimp

Portion Size: 2

Duration: 20 minutes

🛒 Ingredients:
- 12 large shrimp, peeled and deveined
- 2 tablespoons unsalted butter, melted
- 1 clove garlic, minced
- Salt and pepper, to taste
- 1 tablespoon fresh parsley, chopped
- Lemon wedges, for serving

📝 Instructions:

1. **Preheat the Blackstone Griddle** to medium-high heat, aiming for a temperature around 375°F (190°C).

2. **Prepare the Shrimp**: In a mixing bowl, combine the shrimp, melted butter, minced garlic, salt, and pepper. Toss until the shrimp are evenly coated with the garlic butter mixture.

3. **Grill the Shrimp**: Arrange the shrimp on the hot griddle in a single layer. Cook for about 2-3 minutes on each side, or until the shrimp turn pink and opaque, indicating they are fully cooked.

4. **Garnish**: Once cooked, transfer the shrimp to a serving platter. Sprinkle with chopped fresh parsley for added flavor and color.

5. **Serve**: Accompany the grilled garlic butter shrimp with lemon wedges on the side. Squeeze the lemon over the shrimp just before eating for a zesty finish.

Enjoy your Grilled Garlic Butter Shrimp, a simple yet elegant dish that highlights the ease and versatility of cooking with your Blackstone Griddle, perfect for a quick and delicious dinner.

63. Blackstone Griddle-Seared Lamb Chops

🍽 Portion Size: 2
⏳ Duration: 25 minutes

🛒 Ingredients:
- 4 lamb chops, about 1 inch thick
- 2 tablespoons olive oil
- 2 cloves garlic, minced
- 1 teaspoon rosemary, chopped
- 1 teaspoon thyme, chopped
- Salt and pepper, to taste
- 1/4 cup balsamic vinegar
- 1 tablespoon honey

📝 Instructions:

1. **Preparation**: In a small bowl, mix together olive oil, minced garlic, rosemary, thyme, salt, and pepper. Rub this mixture evenly over both sides of the lamb chops. Let them marinate for at least 15 minutes at room temperature to enhance the flavors.

2. **Preheat the Griddle**: Turn your Blackstone griddle to medium-high heat, allowing it to heat up for about 5 minutes. A properly preheated griddle ensures a perfect sear on the lamb chops.

3. **Cook the Lamb Chops**: Place the marinated lamb chops on the hot griddle. Cook for about 4-5 minutes on each side for medium-rare, or adjust the cooking time to achieve your preferred level of doneness.

4. **Balsamic Glaze Preparation**: While the lamb chops are cooking, mix balsamic vinegar and honey in a small bowl.

5. **Apply the Glaze**: In the last minute of cooking, brush the balsamic honey glaze over the lamb chops, flipping them to glaze both sides. This adds a rich, caramelized flavor to the chops.

6. **Rest Before Serving**: Once cooked to your liking, transfer the lamb chops to a plate and let them rest for about 5 minutes. Resting allows the juices to redistribute throughout the meat, ensuring the chops are juicy and flavorful when served.

Serve the lamb chops hot off the griddle, accompanied by your favorite side dishes for a complete meal. Enjoy the rich flavors of the herbs, garlic, and balsamic glaze that make these Blackstone Griddle-Seared Lamb Chops a delightful dining experience.

64. Grilled Balsamic Glazed Steak

Portion Size: 2

Duration: 25 minutes

Ingredients:
- 2 steaks (ribeye or sirloin, about 1 inch thick)
- 1/4 cup balsamic vinegar
- 2 tablespoons olive oil
- 2 cloves garlic, minced
- 1 tablespoon brown sugar
- 1 teaspoon fresh rosemary, chopped (or 1/2 teaspoon dried)
- Salt and pepper, to taste

Instructions:

1. **Marinate the Steaks**: In a small bowl, whisk together balsamic vinegar, olive oil, minced garlic, brown sugar, rosemary, salt, and pepper. Place the steaks in a shallow dish or a resealable plastic bag. Pour the marinade over the steaks, ensuring they are well coated. Marinate in the refrigerator for at least 15 minutes, or up to 2 hours for deeper flavor.

2. **Preheat the Blackstone Griddle**: Turn your Blackstone Griddle to medium-high heat and allow it to preheat for about 5 minutes. A properly preheated griddle ensures even cooking and perfect sear marks.

3. **Grill the Steaks**: Remove the steaks from the marinade, letting excess drip off. Place the steaks on the hot griddle. Cook for about 4-5 minutes on each side for medium-rare, or adjust the cooking time to achieve your preferred level of doneness. Use a meat thermometer to ensure accuracy—135°F for medium-rare, 145°F for medium, 155°F for medium-well.

4. **Rest the Steaks**: Once cooked to your liking, transfer the steaks to a cutting board and let them rest for about 5 minutes. Resting allows the juices to redistribute throughout the meat, ensuring a juicy steak.

5. **Serve**: After resting, slice the steaks against the grain into thin strips. Serve immediately, drizzled with any remaining balsamic glaze from the griddle, if desired. Pair with a side of grilled vegetables or a fresh salad for a complete meal.

65. Griddled Honey Garlic Salmon

Portion Size: 2

Duration: 25 minutes

Ingredients:
- 2 salmon fillets (about 6 oz each)
- 2 tablespoons honey
- 2 tablespoons soy sauce
- 1 tablespoon olive oil
- 3 cloves garlic, minced
- 1 teaspoon fresh ginger, grated
- Salt and pepper, to taste
- Lemon wedges, for serving
- Fresh parsley, chopped, for garnish

Instructions:

1. **Marinate the Salmon**: In a small bowl, whisk together honey, soy sauce, minced garlic, and grated ginger. Season the salmon fillets with salt and pepper on both sides. Place the salmon in a shallow dish or a resealable plastic bag. Pour the marinade over the salmon, ensuring each fillet is well coated. Let marinate for at least 15 minutes in the refrigerator.

2. **Preheat the Griddle**: Turn your Blackstone griddle to medium-high heat, allowing it to warm up for about 5 minutes. A properly preheated griddle ensures the salmon will cook evenly and get a nice sear.

3. **Cook the Salmon**: Remove the salmon from the marinade, reserving the excess marinade. Lightly oil the griddle surface with olive oil. Place the salmon fillets on the griddle, skin side down, and cook for about 4-5 minutes. Carefully flip the fillets and cook for an additional 4-5 minutes on the other side, or until the salmon is cooked through and easily flakes with a fork.

4. **Reduce the Marinade**: While the salmon is cooking, pour the reserved marinade into a small pan. Place it on the griddle and bring to a simmer. Cook until the sauce thickens slightly, about 3-4 minutes. This will be used as a glaze for the salmon.

5. **Serve**: Once the salmon is cooked, transfer the fillets to a serving plate. Drizzle the reduced marinade over the salmon. Garnish with fresh parsley and serve with lemon wedges on the side.

Enjoy your Griddled Honey Garlic Salmon, a simple yet flavorful dish that highlights the ease and versatility of cooking with your Blackstone Griddle.

66. Grilled Cajun Chicken Alfredo

Portion Size: 2

Duration: 30 minutes

Ingredients:

- 2 boneless, skinless chicken breasts
- 2 tablespoons Cajun seasoning

- 1 tablespoon olive oil
- 8 oz fettuccine pasta
- 2 tablespoons unsalted butter
- 1 cup heavy cream
- 1 cup grated Parmesan cheese
- Salt, to taste
- Freshly ground black pepper, to taste
- 2 tablespoons chopped parsley, for garnish
- Lemon wedges, for serving

Instructions:

1. **Season the Chicken**: Rub the chicken breasts evenly with Cajun seasoning, ensuring both sides are well-coated.

2. **Preheat the Blackstone Griddle**: Turn your Blackstone griddle to medium-high heat, allowing it to warm up for about 5 minutes.

3. **Cook the Chicken**: Drizzle olive oil over the hot griddle. Place the seasoned chicken breasts on the griddle and cook for about 5-7 minutes on each side, or until the internal temperature reaches 165°F (74°C) and they have a nice charred exterior. Remove the chicken from the griddle and let it rest for a few minutes before slicing it thinly.

4. **Boil the Pasta**: While the chicken is cooking, bring a large pot of salted water to a boil. Add the fettuccine and cook according to the package instructions until al dente. Drain the pasta and set aside.

5. **Prepare the Alfredo Sauce**: Lower the griddle heat to medium. Add butter to the griddle, allowing it to melt. Stir in the heavy cream and bring to a simmer. Let it simmer for 2-3 minutes, stirring frequently, until the cream starts to thicken.

6. **Combine Sauce and Pasta**: Add the grated Parmesan cheese to the cream mixture, stirring until the cheese is melted and the sauce is smooth. Season with salt and pepper to taste. Add the cooked pasta to the sauce, tossing to coat the pasta evenly in the Alfredo sauce.

7. **Serve**: Place a portion of the creamy fettuccine Alfredo on each plate. Top with sliced Cajun chicken. Garnish with chopped parsley and serve with lemon wedges on the side.

Enjoy your Grilled Cajun Chicken Alfredo, a perfect blend of spicy, charred chicken and creamy pasta, made easy on your Blackstone Griddle.

67. Griddled BBQ Chicken Breasts

Portion Size: 2

Duration: 25 minutes

Ingredients:
- 2 boneless, skinless chicken breasts
- 1/4 cup BBQ sauce, plus extra for serving
- Salt and pepper, to taste
- 1 tablespoon olive oil
- Optional garnishes: chopped fresh parsley or cilantro, and sliced green onions

Instructions:

1. **Preheat the Blackstone Griddle** to medium-high heat, aiming for a surface temperature of around 375°F (190°C).

2. **Prepare the Chicken**: Season both sides of the chicken breasts with salt and pepper. Brush each breast with BBQ sauce, ensuring they are well coated.

3. **Griddle the Chicken**: Drizzle olive oil onto the griddle surface to prevent sticking. Place the chicken breasts on the griddle and cook for about 6-7 minutes on each side, or until the internal temperature reaches 165°F (74°C) and they have nice grill marks.

4. **Baste with BBQ Sauce**: Halfway through cooking, baste the chicken with additional BBQ sauce, flipping and applying sauce to both sides to build up a rich glaze.

5. **Rest the Chicken**: Once cooked, transfer the chicken breasts to a cutting board and let them rest for about 5 minutes. This allows the juices to redistribute, ensuring the chicken is juicy and flavorful.

6. **Serve**: Slice the chicken breasts against the grain into strips. Serve hot, garnished with optional chopped parsley, cilantro, or sliced green onions, and accompanied by extra BBQ sauce on the side.

Enjoy your Griddled BBQ Chicken Breasts, a simple yet delicious centerpiece for a quick and satisfying meal, perfectly complementing the ease and versatility of cooking with your Blackstone Griddle.

68. Grilled Chimichurri Flank Steak

Portion Size: 2

Duration: 25 minutes

Ingredients:
- 1 lb flank steak
- 1/2 cup fresh parsley, finely chopped
- 1/4 cup olive oil
- 3 tablespoons red wine vinegar
- 3 cloves garlic, minced
- 1 teaspoon red chili flakes
- 1 teaspoon dried oregano
- Salt and pepper to taste
- Additional olive oil for grilling

Instructions:

1. **Prepare the Chimichurri Sauce**: In a bowl, combine the chopped parsley, olive oil, red wine vinegar, minced garlic, red chili flakes, dried oregano, salt, and pepper. Mix well until all ingredients are evenly distributed. Set aside half of the sauce for serving and use the other half for marinating the steak.

2. **Marinate the Steak**: Place the flank steak in a shallow dish or a resealable plastic bag. Pour half of the chimichurri sauce over the steak, ensuring it is well coated. Marinate in the refrigerator for at least 15 minutes, or up to 2 hours for deeper flavor.

3. **Preheat the Blackstone Griddle**: Turn your Blackstone griddle to high heat, allowing it to preheat for about 5 minutes. A properly heated griddle ensures a good sear on the steak.

4. **Grill the Steak**: Remove the steak from the marinade, letting excess sauce drip off. Lightly oil the griddle surface with additional olive oil. Place the steak on the griddle and cook for about 5-7 minutes on each side for medium-rare, or adjust the cooking time to achieve your preferred level of doneness. Season with additional salt and pepper while grilling if desired.

5. **Rest the Steak**: Once cooked to your liking, transfer the steak to a cutting board and let it rest for 5 minutes. This allows the juices to redistribute throughout the meat, ensuring it is juicy and flavorful.

6. **Slice and Serve**: Slice the steak against the grain into thin strips. Serve the sliced steak with the reserved chimichurri sauce drizzled on top or on the side for dipping.

Enjoy your Grilled Chimichurri Flank Steak, a flavorful and easy-to-prepare meal perfect for any outdoor grilling occasion.

69. Blackstone Griddle-Cooked Stuffed Bell Peppers

Portion Size: 2
Duration: 45 minutes

Ingredients:
- 2 large bell peppers, halved and deseeded
- 1/2 lb ground beef
- 1/4 cup onion, finely chopped
- 1 garlic clove, minced
- 1/2 cup cooked rice
- 1 cup canned diced tomatoes, drained
- 1 teaspoon salt
- 1/2 teaspoon black pepper
- 1/2 teaspoon smoked paprika
- 1/4 cup shredded cheddar cheese
- 1 tablespoon olive oil
- Fresh parsley, for garnish

Instructions:
1. Preheat your Blackstone griddle to medium heat, around 350°F (175°C).

2. In a large bowl, mix together ground beef, onion, garlic, cooked rice, diced tomatoes, salt, pepper, and smoked paprika until well combined.

3. Fill each bell pepper half with the beef and rice mixture, pressing down slightly to pack it in.

4. Brush the stuffed bell peppers lightly with olive oil on the outside to prevent sticking and to enhance flavor.

5. Place the stuffed bell peppers on the griddle, cut side up. Cook for about 25-30 minutes with the griddle lid closed, or until the peppers are tender and the filling is cooked through. If your griddle doesn't have a lid, cover the peppers with a large metal bowl or aluminum foil to create a similar cooking environment.

6. In the last 5 minutes of cooking, sprinkle shredded cheddar cheese over the top of each stuffed pepper. Continue cooking until the cheese is melted and bubbly.

7. Carefully remove the stuffed bell peppers from the griddle using a spatula.

8. Garnish with fresh parsley before serving.

Enjoy your Blackstone Griddle-Cooked Stuffed Bell Peppers, a delicious and straightforward dish that brings out the smoky flavors of outdoor grilling, perfect for a cozy dinner.

70. Griddled Lemon Dill Tilapia

Portion Size: 2

Duration: 20 minutes

Ingredients:
- 2 tilapia fillets
- 2 tablespoons olive oil
- Salt and pepper, to taste
- 1 teaspoon dried dill
- 1 lemon, sliced into thin rounds
- Additional lemon wedges, for serving

Instructions:

1. **Preheat the Blackstone Griddle** to medium-high heat, aiming for a surface temperature of around 375°F (190°C).

2. **Prepare the Tilapia**: Pat the tilapia fillets dry with paper towels. Brush both sides of each fillet with olive oil, then season with salt, pepper, and dried dill.

3. **Griddle the Lemon**: Before cooking the tilapia, place lemon slices on the griddle for about 1 minute on each side, or until they are lightly charred. Remove and set aside.

4. **Cook the Tilapia**: Place the seasoned tilapia fillets on the griddle. Cook for about 3-4 minutes on one side, until the edges start to turn opaque. Carefully flip the fillets with a spatula and cook for another 3-4 minutes on the other side, or until the fish flakes easily with a fork and reaches an internal temperature of 145°F (63°C).

5. **Serve**: Transfer the cooked tilapia fillets to plates. Garnish with the grilled lemon slices and serve with additional lemon wedges on the side.

Enjoy your Griddled Lemon Dill Tilapia, a simple yet flavorful dish that highlights the ease of cooking with your Blackstone Griddle.

71. Grilled Teriyaki Pork Chops

Portion Size: 2

Duration: 25 minutes

Ingredients:
- 2 pork chops, about 1 inch thick
- 1/4 cup soy sauce
- 2 tablespoons brown sugar
- 1 tablespoon olive oil, plus more for griddling

- 2 cloves garlic, minced
- 1 teaspoon ginger, grated
- 1 tablespoon rice vinegar
- 1 teaspoon sesame oil
- Salt and pepper, to taste
- Optional: Sesame seeds and sliced green onions for garnish

Instructions:

1. **Marinate the Pork Chops**: In a mixing bowl, whisk together soy sauce, brown sugar, 1 tablespoon olive oil, minced garlic, grated ginger, rice vinegar, and sesame oil until the sugar is fully dissolved. Season the pork chops with salt and pepper, then place them in a large resealable plastic bag. Pour the marinade over the pork chops, seal the bag, and ensure the chops are well coated. Marinate in the refrigerator for at least 1 hour, or up to 4 hours for deeper flavor.

2. **Preheat the Blackstone Griddle**: Remove the pork chops from the refrigerator and let them come to room temperature for about 15 minutes. Meanwhile, heat your Blackstone griddle over medium-high heat. Lightly oil the griddle surface with olive oil.

3. **Griddle the Pork Chops**: Remove the pork chops from the marinade, letting any excess drip off. Discard the remaining marinade. Place the pork chops on the hot griddle and cook for about 5-7 minutes on each side, or until they reach an internal temperature of 145°F (63°C) and have nice grill marks.

4. **Rest the Pork Chops**: Transfer the cooked pork chops to a plate and let them rest for 5 minutes. This allows the juices to redistribute throughout the meat, ensuring a moist and tender chop.

5. **Serve**: Slice the pork chops against the grain for tenderness. Optionally, sprinkle sesame seeds and sliced green onions over the top for garnish. Serve immediately with your choice of side dishes.

Enjoy your Grilled Teriyaki Pork Chops, a flavorful and easy-to-prepare meal perfect for any outdoor grilling occasion on your Blackstone Griddle.

72. Griddled Mushroom and Swiss Burger

Portion Size: 2

Duration: 30 minutes

Ingredients:

- 2 burger patties (about 6 oz each)
- 4 large Portobello mushrooms, stems removed
- 4 slices of Swiss cheese
- 1 tablespoon olive oil
- Salt and pepper, to taste
- 1/2 red onion, thinly sliced
- 4 tablespoons mayonnaise
- 2 tablespoons Dijon mustard
- 4 leaves of lettuce
- 2 brioche buns, split

Instructions:

1. **Preheat the Blackstone Griddle** to medium-high heat, around 375°F (190°C).

2. **Prepare the Mushrooms**: Brush both sides of the Portobello mushrooms with olive oil and season with salt and pepper. Set aside.

3. **Cook the Burgers**: Place the burger patties on the griddle. Season with salt and pepper. Cook for about 4-5 minutes per side, or until they reach your desired level of doneness. In the last minute of cooking, place a slice of Swiss cheese on each patty to melt.

4. **Grill the Mushrooms**: While the burgers are cooking, place the Portobello mushrooms on the griddle, gill side down. Grill for about 4 minutes, then flip and cook for another 4 minutes, or until tender. Remove from the griddle and keep warm.

5. **Sauté the Onions**: In the same griddle, add the sliced red onions and cook for about 5-7 minutes, stirring occasionally, until caramelized and soft. Remove from the griddle and set aside.

6. **Prepare the Buns**: Toast the brioche buns on the griddle for about 1-2 minutes, or until lightly golden and crispy.

7. **Assemble the Burgers**: Spread mayonnaise and Dijon mustard on the bottom halves of the toasted brioche buns. Place a lettuce leaf on each bottom bun, followed by a grilled Portobello mushroom. Add the cheese-topped burger patty on top of the mushroom and then some caramelized onions. Cover with the top halves of the buns.

8. **Serve Immediately**: Enjoy your Griddled Mushroom and Swiss Burger hot off the griddle, accompanied by your favorite side dish or a crisp salad.

73. Grilled Thai Peanut Chicken Skewers

Portion Size: 2

Duration: 30 minutes

Ingredients:

- 1 lb chicken breasts, cut into 1-inch cubes
- 1/4 cup creamy peanut butter
- 2 tablespoons soy sauce
- 1 tablespoon lime juice
- 1 tablespoon honey
- 2 cloves garlic, minced
- 1 teaspoon grated ginger
- 1/2 teaspoon crushed red pepper flakes (adjust to taste)
- 1 tablespoon vegetable oil
- Wooden skewers, soaked in water for at least 30 minutes
- Optional garnish: chopped cilantro, chopped peanuts, lime wedges

Instructions:

1. **Marinate the Chicken**: In a mixing bowl, whisk together peanut butter, soy sauce, lime juice, honey, minced garlic, grated ginger, and crushed red pepper flakes until smooth. Add the chicken cubes to the bowl and toss to coat evenly with the marinade. Cover and refrigerate for at least 15 minutes, or up to 2 hours for deeper flavor.

2. **Preheat the Blackstone Griddle**: Turn your Blackstone Griddle to medium-high heat, allowing it to preheat for about 5 minutes. A properly preheated griddle ensures even cooking and perfect grill marks.

3. **Prepare the Skewers**: Thread the marinated chicken cubes onto the soaked wooden skewers, leaving a small space between each piece to ensure even cooking.

4. **Grill the Skewers**: Brush the griddle with vegetable oil to prevent sticking. Place the chicken skewers on the griddle and cook for about 4-5 minutes on each side, or until the chicken is fully cooked through and has a nice char on the outside. The internal temperature of the chicken should reach 165°F.

5. **Serve**: Once cooked, transfer the skewers to a serving platter. Optionally, garnish with chopped cilantro, chopped peanuts, and lime wedges on the side. Serve immediately, offering a burst of Thai flavors that complement the tender, grilled chicken.

Enjoy your Grilled Thai Peanut Chicken Skewers, a dish that brings the exotic flavors of Thailand to your backyard, perfectly crafted on your Blackstone Griddle for a quick and delicious dinner.

74. Griddle-Cooked Chicken Fajita Quesadillas

Portion Size: 2

Duration: 25 minutes

Ingredients:
- 2 large chicken breasts, thinly sliced
- 1 tablespoon olive oil
- 1 teaspoon chili powder
- 1 teaspoon cumin
- 1/2 teaspoon garlic powder
- Salt and pepper to taste
- 1 large bell pepper, sliced
- 1 large onion, sliced
- 4 large flour tortillas
- 1 cup shredded cheddar cheese
- Optional garnishes: sour cream, salsa, guacamole

Instructions:
1. **Season the Chicken**: In a bowl, combine the sliced chicken breasts with olive oil, chili powder, cumin, garlic powder, salt, and pepper. Toss until the chicken is evenly coated.

2. **Preheat the Griddle**: Turn your Blackstone griddle to medium-high heat, allowing it to warm up for about 5 minutes.

3. **Cook the Chicken**: Place the seasoned chicken slices onto the hot griddle. Cook for about 5-7 minutes, turning occasionally, until the chicken is fully cooked and slightly charred on the edges. Transfer the cooked chicken to a plate and set aside.

4. **Griddle the Vegetables**: In the same griddle, add the sliced bell pepper and onion. Season with a pinch of salt and pepper. Cook for about 5-7 minutes, stirring occasionally, until the vegetables are soft and have a slight char. Remove from the griddle and set aside with the chicken.

5. Assemble the Quesadillas: Lay out the flour tortillas on a clean surface. Sprinkle half of the cheese evenly over two tortillas. Then, evenly distribute the cooked chicken and vegetables over the cheese. Sprinkle the remaining cheese on top of the chicken and vegetables, and cover each with another tortilla.

6. Cook the Quesadillas: Carefully transfer the assembled quesadillas back to the griddle. Cook for about 2-3 minutes on each side, or until the tortillas are golden brown and crispy, and the cheese has melted. Use a spatula to press down gently on the quesadillas as they cook to ensure even contact with the griddle.

7. Serve: Once cooked, transfer the quesadillas to a cutting board. Let them cool for 1-2 minutes before slicing each quesadilla into wedges. Serve with optional garnishes such as sour cream, salsa, and guacamole on the side.

Enjoy your Griddle-Cooked Chicken Fajita Quesadillas, a flavorful and satisfying meal that brings the best of Blackstone griddle cooking to your table.

75. Grilled Pineapple Teriyaki Chicken

Portion Size: 2

Duration: 30 minutes

Ingredients:
- 2 boneless, skinless chicken breasts
- 1 cup pineapple, sliced into 1/2-inch rounds
- 1/4 cup teriyaki sauce, plus more for glazing
- 1 tablespoon olive oil
- Salt and pepper, to taste
- 2 cups cooked rice, for serving
- Optional: sesame seeds and sliced green onions for garnish

Instructions:

1. **Preheat the Blackstone Griddle** to medium-high heat, around 375°F (190°C).

2. **Prepare the Chicken**: Season both sides of the chicken breasts with salt and pepper. Brush each breast with teriyaki sauce, ensuring they are well coated.

3. **Grill the Chicken**: Lightly oil the griddle surface with olive oil. Place the chicken breasts on the griddle and cook for about 6-7 minutes per side, or until the internal temperature reaches 165°F (74°C) and they have nice grill marks. During the last 2 minutes of cooking, brush additional teriyaki sauce over the chicken for extra flavor.

4. **Grill the Pineapple**: While the chicken is cooking, place the pineapple slices on the griddle. Grill for about 2-3 minutes per side, or until they are caramelized and have grill marks.

5. **Rest and Slice the Chicken**: Once cooked, transfer the chicken to a cutting board and let it rest for a few minutes. Then, slice the chicken breasts against the grain into thin strips.

6. **Serve**: Divide the cooked rice between two plates. Top with sliced chicken and grilled pineapple. If desired, garnish with sesame seeds and sliced green onions.

Enjoy your Grilled Pineapple Teriyaki Chicken, a flavorful and easy-to-make dish that perfectly embodies the simplicity and joy of griddle cooking, making it a delightful addition to your dinner repertoire.

76. Griddled Rosemary Garlic Pork Tenderloin

Portion Size: 2

Duration: 30 minutes

Ingredients:
- 2 pork tenderloins (about 1 lb each)
- 2 tablespoons olive oil
- 4 garlic cloves, minced
- 2 tablespoons fresh rosemary, finely chopped
- Salt and pepper, to taste
- 1/4 cup balsamic vinegar
- 1/4 cup chicken broth

Instructions:

1. **Preheat the Blackstone Griddle** to medium-high heat, aiming for a surface temperature of around 400°F.

2. **Prepare the Pork Tenderloins**: Trim any excess fat from the pork tenderloins. In a small bowl, mix together the olive oil, minced garlic, chopped rosemary, salt, and pepper. Rub this mixture all over the pork tenderloins, ensuring they are well coated.

3. **Grill the Pork Tenderloins**: Place the seasoned pork tenderloins on the hot griddle. Cook for about 7-8 minutes on each side, or until the internal temperature reaches 145°F for medium-rare. Use a meat thermometer to ensure accuracy.

4. **Make the Balsamic Glaze**: While the pork is cooking, mix the balsamic vinegar and chicken broth in a small bowl. After the pork has been turned once and is about halfway through cooking on the second side, pour the balsamic mixture over the tenderloins on the griddle. Allow the mixture to bubble and reduce, forming a glaze over the pork, for the remaining cooking time.

5. **Rest the Pork**: Once cooked to the desired doneness, remove the pork tenderloins from the griddle and let them rest for 5 minutes. This allows the juices to redistribute throughout the meat, ensuring it will be moist and flavorful.

6. **Serve**: Slice the pork tenderloins into medallions. Drizzle any remaining glaze from the griddle over the slices. Serve immediately, accompanied by your choice of side dishes.

Enjoy your Griddled Rosemary Garlic Pork Tenderloin, a flavorful and elegant meal that showcases the ease and versatility of cooking with your Blackstone Griddle.

77. Grilled Jerk Chicken with Pineapple Salsa

Portion Size: 2

Duration: 45 minutes

Ingredients:

- 2 boneless, skinless chicken breasts
- 2 tablespoons jerk seasoning paste
- 1 tablespoon olive oil
- Salt to taste

- **For the Pineapple Salsa:**
  - 1 cup diced fresh pineapple
  - 1/4 cup diced red bell pepper
  - 1/4 cup diced red onion
  - 1 jalapeño, seeded and finely chopped (adjust based on heat preference)
  - 2 tablespoons chopped fresh cilantro
  - Juice of 1 lime
  - Salt to taste

Instructions:

1. **Prep the Chicken**: Rub each chicken breast with the jerk seasoning paste, ensuring they are well coated. Drizzle with olive oil and season with salt to taste. Let marinate for at least 15 minutes, or up to 1 hour in the refrigerator for deeper flavor.

2. **Preheat the Blackstone Griddle**: Turn your Blackstone griddle to medium-high heat, allowing it to warm up for about 5 minutes.

3. **Grill the Chicken**: Place the marinated chicken breasts on the hot griddle. Cook for about 6-7 minutes on each side, or until the internal temperature reaches 165°F (74°C) and the outside is nicely charred. Once cooked, transfer the chicken to a cutting board and let it rest for a few minutes before slicing.

4. **Prepare the Pineapple Salsa**: While the chicken is cooking, combine diced pineapple, red bell pepper, red onion, jalapeño, and cilantro in a medium bowl. Add lime juice and salt to taste. Mix well to combine. Adjust seasoning and lime juice according to taste.

5. **Serve**: Slice the rested jerk chicken and serve it on a plate. Spoon a generous amount of pineapple salsa over the chicken or alongside it.

Enjoy your Grilled Jerk Chicken with Pineapple Salsa, a vibrant and flavorful dish that brings a taste of the Caribbean to your table with the ease of your Blackstone Griddle.

78. Blackstone Griddle-Seared Scallops with Garlic Butter

Portion Size: 2

Duration: 20 minutes

Ingredients:
- 10 large sea scallops, patted dry
- 2 tablespoons unsalted butter
- 2 cloves garlic, minced
- Salt and freshly ground black pepper, to taste
- 1 tablespoon olive oil
- 1 lemon, for garnish
- Fresh parsley, chopped, for garnish

Instructions:

1. **Preheat the Blackstone Griddle** over medium-high heat. Aim for a surface temperature of around 400°F (204°C) to ensure a good sear on the scallops.

2. **Season the Scallops**: Lightly season the scallops on both sides with salt and freshly ground black pepper.

3. **Prepare the Garlic Butter**: In a small bowl, melt the unsalted butter. Mix in the minced garlic to the melted butter and set aside.

4. **Cook the Scallops**: Drizzle olive oil onto the hot griddle. Carefully place the scallops on the griddle, ensuring they are not touching. Cook for about 2 minutes on one side, or until a golden crust forms.

5. **Flip the Scallops**: Gently flip each scallop using tongs or a spatula. Cook for an additional 1-2 minutes on the other side.

6. **Add Garlic Butter**: Spoon the garlic butter mixture over each scallop while they are still on the griddle. Allow the scallops to cook in the garlic butter for an additional minute, basting them with the butter.

7. **Garnish and Serve**: Remove the scallops from the griddle and place them on a serving plate. Squeeze fresh lemon juice over the scallops and garnish with chopped parsley. Serve immediately while hot.

Enjoy your Blackstone Griddle-Seared Scallops with Garlic Butter, a simple yet elegant dish that highlights the natural sweetness of the scallops, enhanced by the richness of garlic butter.

79. Griddled Sweet and Spicy BBQ Ribs

Portion Size: 2

Duration: 60 minutes

Ingredients:

- 2 lbs baby back ribs
- 2 tablespoons olive oil
- 1 tablespoon kosher salt
- 1 tablespoon ground black pepper
- 1 tablespoon smoked paprika
- 2 teaspoons garlic powder
- 2 teaspoons onion powder
- 1 cup BBQ sauce (sweet and spicy variety)
- 1/4 cup honey
- 1/4 cup apple cider vinegar
- Optional: 1 teaspoon red pepper flakes for extra heat

Instructions:

1. **Prepare the Ribs**: Remove the membrane from the back of the ribs by sliding a knife under the membrane and pulling it away. This step is crucial for tender ribs.

2. **Season the Ribs**: Rub both sides of the ribs with olive oil. In a small bowl, mix together the salt, black pepper, smoked paprika, garlic powder, and onion powder. Sprinkle the seasoning mix evenly over the ribs, pressing gently to adhere.

3. **Preheat the Blackstone Griddle**: Turn your Blackstone Griddle to low heat, aiming for a temperature around 225°F to 250°F (107°C to 121°C). This low and slow approach is key for perfectly cooked ribs.

4. **Cook the Ribs**: Place the ribs on the griddle, meaty side up. Close the lid if your griddle model has one, or cover the ribs with a large inverted aluminum pan to create an oven-like environment. Cook for about 1 hour, checking occasionally to ensure they are cooking evenly.

5. **Make the Glaze**: While the ribs are cooking, mix the BBQ sauce, honey, apple cider vinegar, and optional red pepper flakes in a bowl. This sweet and spicy glaze will be brushed on the ribs later.

6. **Glaze the Ribs**: After 1 hour, increase the griddle temperature to medium heat (around 350°F or 177°C). Brush the ribs generously with the BBQ glaze on both sides. Cook for an additional 15-20 minutes, flipping once and reapplying the glaze to caramelize it onto the ribs.

7. **Rest the Ribs**: Remove the ribs from the griddle and let them rest for about 10 minutes. This allows the juices to redistribute, making the ribs even more tender.

8. **Serve**: Cut the ribs between the bones, plate, and serve with additional BBQ sauce on the side if desired.

Enjoy your Griddled Sweet and Spicy BBQ Ribs, a centerpiece dish that showcases your griddle cooking skills with a classic American BBQ flavor.

80. Grilled Honey Sriracha Chicken Thighs

Portion Size: 2

Duration: 25 minutes

Ingredients:
- 4 chicken thighs, boneless and skinless
- 2 tablespoons honey
- 1 tablespoon Sriracha sauce
- 1 tablespoon soy sauce
- 1 tablespoon olive oil
- 1 teaspoon garlic, minced
- Salt and pepper, to taste
- Optional garnish: sesame seeds and sliced green onions

Instructions:

1. **Preparation**: In a mixing bowl, combine honey, Sriracha sauce, soy sauce, olive oil, and minced garlic. Season with salt and pepper to taste. Stir well to create the marinade.

2. **Marinate Chicken**: Add the chicken thighs to the marinade, ensuring each piece is well-coated. Let them marinate for at least 15 minutes, or for better flavor, cover and refrigerate for up to 2 hours.

3. **Preheat the Griddle**: Turn your Blackstone griddle to medium-high heat, allowing it to heat up for about 5 minutes. A properly preheated griddle ensures even cooking and perfect caramelization.

4. **Grill the Chicken**: Remove the chicken thighs from the marinade, letting any excess drip off. Place the chicken on the griddle and cook for about 6-7 minutes on each side, or until the chicken is thoroughly cooked and the internal temperature reaches 165°F (74°C). Baste the chicken with the remaining marinade during the last few minutes of cooking for extra flavor.

5. **Rest the Chicken**: Once cooked, transfer the chicken thighs to a plate and let them rest for a few minutes. This step allows the juices to redistribute, ensuring the chicken is juicy and flavorful.

6. **Serve**: Slice the chicken thighs and serve on a platter. Garnish with sesame seeds and sliced green onions if desired. Enjoy your Grilled Honey Sriracha Chicken Thighs with a side of steamed rice or vegetables for a complete meal.

81. Griddled Herb-Crusted Salmon Fillets

Portion Size: 2

Duration: 25 minutes

Ingredients:
- 2 salmon fillets (about 6 oz each)
- 1 tablespoon olive oil
- Salt and pepper, to taste
- 1 teaspoon dried rosemary
- 1 teaspoon dried thyme
- 1 teaspoon dried oregano
- 1 teaspoon garlic powder
- Lemon wedges, for serving

Instructions:

1. **Preheat the Blackstone Griddle** to medium-high heat, aiming for a temperature around 375°F (190°C).

2. **Prepare the Herb Crust Mixture**: In a small bowl, combine the dried rosemary, thyme, oregano, and garlic powder. Mix well to create the herb crust seasoning.

3. **Season the Salmon**: Brush both sides of the salmon fillets with olive oil. Season generously with salt and pepper. Sprinkle the herb crust mixture evenly over the top side of each salmon fillet, pressing gently to adhere.

4. **Griddle the Salmon**: Place the salmon fillets on the griddle, herb side down, and cook for about 4-5 minutes until the herbs are slightly charred and aromatic. Carefully flip the salmon fillets using a spatula and cook for an additional 3-4 minutes on the other side, or until the salmon reaches your desired level of doneness.

5. **Serve**: Transfer the griddled herb-crusted salmon fillets to plates. Serve immediately with lemon wedges on the side for squeezing over the salmon.

Enjoy your Griddled Herb-Crusted Salmon Fillets, a flavorful and elegant dish that's simple to prepare on your Blackstone Griddle, perfect for a quick yet sophisticated dinner.

82. Grilled Mediterranean Lamb Kebabs

Portion Size: 2

Duration: 30 minutes

Ingredients:
- 1 lb lamb, cut into 1-inch cubes
- 2 tablespoons olive oil
- 2 cloves garlic, minced
- 1 teaspoon dried oregano
- 1 teaspoon ground cumin
- 1/2 teaspoon paprika
- Salt and pepper, to taste

- 1 lemon, juiced
- 1 red onion, cut into 1-inch pieces
- 1 bell pepper, cut into 1-inch pieces
- Wooden or metal skewers (if using wooden skewers, soak in water for at least 30 minutes before grilling)

Instructions:

1. In a large bowl, combine olive oil, minced garlic, dried oregano, ground cumin, paprika, salt, pepper, and lemon juice. Stir to create a marinade.

2. Add the lamb cubes to the marinade, ensuring each piece is well-coated. Cover and refrigerate for at least 2 hours, or overnight for best flavor.

3. Preheat your Blackstone griddle to medium-high heat, around 375°F (190°C).

4. Thread the marinated lamb cubes onto skewers, alternating with pieces of red onion and bell pepper.

5. Place the skewers on the hot griddle. Grill for about 10-12 minutes, turning occasionally, until the lamb is cooked to your desired doneness and vegetables are slightly charred.

6. Remove the skewers from the griddle and let them rest for a few minutes before serving.

Enjoy your Grilled Mediterranean Lamb Kebabs, a flavorful and easy-to-prepare dish perfect for any outdoor grilling occasion.

83. Griddled Blackened Catfish

Portion Size: 2

Duration: 20 minutes

Ingredients:

- 2 catfish fillets (about 6-8 ounces each)
- 2 tablespoons olive oil
- 1 tablespoon paprika
- 1 teaspoon garlic powder
- 1 teaspoon onion powder
- 1 teaspoon dried thyme
- 1 teaspoon dried oregano
- 1/2 teaspoon cayenne pepper (adjust to taste)
- 1/2 teaspoon salt
- 1/2 teaspoon black pepper
- Lemon wedges, for serving

Instructions:

1. **Prepare the Seasoning Mix**: In a small bowl, combine paprika, garlic powder, onion powder, dried thyme, dried oregano, cayenne pepper, salt, and black pepper. Mix well to create the blackening seasoning.

2. **Season the Catfish**: Drizzle each catfish fillet with 1 tablespoon of olive oil, ensuring both sides are coated. Rub the blackening seasoning onto both sides of the catfish fillets, pressing it into the fish to adhere.

3. **Preheat the Blackstone Griddle**: Turn your Blackstone Griddle to medium-high heat, allowing it to reach a temperature of around 400°F. This ensures a nice sear and crust on the catfish.

4. **Griddle the Catfish**: Once the griddle is hot, place the seasoned catfish fillets on the surface. Cook for about 3-4 minutes on each side, or until the fish is opaque and flakes easily with a fork. The seasoning should form a slightly charred crust.

5. **Serve**: Remove the catfish from the griddle and let it rest for a couple of minutes. Serve hot with lemon wedges on the side for squeezing over the fish.

Enjoy your Griddled Blackened Catfish, a flavorful and easy-to-prepare meal that brings the essence of outdoor cooking to your dinner table with the ease of your Blackstone Griddle.

84. Grilled Hoisin Glazed Pork Ribs

Portion Size: 2

Duration: 1 hour

Ingredients:

- 2 lbs pork ribs
- 1/4 cup hoisin sauce
- 2 tablespoons soy sauce
- 2 tablespoons honey
- 1 tablespoon rice vinegar
- 2 cloves garlic, minced
- 1 teaspoon ginger, grated
- 1 teaspoon sesame oil
- Salt and pepper, to taste
- Optional: sesame seeds and sliced green onions for garnish

Instructions:

1. **Prepare the Ribs**: If not already done, remove the membrane from the back of the ribs by sliding a knife under the membrane and pulling it away with a paper towel for a better grip.

2. **Season the Ribs**: Lightly season both sides of the ribs with salt and pepper.

3. **Make the Hoisin Glaze**: In a bowl, whisk together hoisin sauce, soy sauce, honey, rice vinegar, minced garlic, grated ginger, and sesame oil until well combined.

4. **Apply the Glaze**: Brush both sides of the ribs generously with the hoisin glaze. Reserve some glaze for basting during cooking.

5. **Preheat the Blackstone Griddle**: Turn your Blackstone Griddle to low-medium heat, aiming for a temperature around 300°F (150°C). Allow it to preheat for about 5 minutes.

6. **Grill the Ribs**: Place the ribs on the griddle, meaty side down. Close the lid of the griddle if available, or cover the ribs with aluminum foil to create an oven-like environment. Cook for about 20 minutes.

7. **Flip and Baste**: Carefully flip the ribs over, baste with the reserved glaze, and cover again. Continue cooking for another 20 minutes, basting occasionally with more glaze.

8. **Check for Doneness**: The ribs are done when the meat is tender and easily pulls away from the bone. If not tender, continue cooking, checking every 10 minutes.

9. **Final Glaze and Serve**: Once the ribs are cooked to your liking, apply a final coat of the hoisin glaze, and increase the heat to medium-high for 2-3 minutes to caramelize the outside. Remove from the griddle and let rest for 5 minutes.

10. **Garnish and Enjoy**: Slice the ribs between the bones, garnish with sesame seeds and sliced green onions if desired, and serve hot.

Enjoy your Grilled Hoisin Glazed Pork Ribs, a flavorful and succulent dish that showcases your griddle cooking skills with an Asian-inspired twist.

85. Griddled Italian Chicken Cutlets

Portion Size: 2

Duration: 25 minutes

Ingredients:
- 2 boneless, skinless chicken breasts
- 1 tablespoon olive oil
- 1 teaspoon Italian seasoning
- 1/2 teaspoon garlic powder
- Salt and pepper, to taste
- 1/2 cup all-purpose flour
- 2 eggs, beaten
- 1 cup breadcrumbs
- 1/2 cup grated Parmesan cheese
- 2 tablespoons unsalted butter
- 1 lemon, cut into wedges for serving
- Fresh parsley, chopped for garnish

Instructions:
1. **Prepare the Chicken**: Place each chicken breast between two pieces of plastic wrap. Use a meat mallet or rolling pin to pound them to an even thickness of about 1/2 inch. This ensures even cooking.

2. **Season the Chicken**: In a small bowl, mix together the olive oil, Italian seasoning, garlic powder, salt, and pepper. Brush this mixture over both sides of the chicken breasts.

3. **Dredge the Chicken**: Place the flour, beaten eggs, and breadcrumbs mixed with grated Parmesan cheese in three separate shallow dishes. Dredge each chicken breast in flour, shaking off the excess. Dip in the beaten eggs, then coat with the breadcrumb mixture, pressing to adhere.

4. **Preheat the Griddle**: Heat your Blackstone griddle over medium-high heat. Once hot, add the butter and let it melt, swirling to coat the surface.

5. **Cook the Chicken**: Place the breaded chicken cutlets on the griddle. Cook for about 4-5 minutes on each side, or until golden brown and the internal temperature reaches 165°F. The exact cooking time may vary depending on the thickness of the chicken.

6. **Serve**: Transfer the cooked chicken cutlets to plates. Squeeze fresh lemon juice over each cutlet and garnish with chopped parsley. Serve immediately.

Enjoy your Griddled Italian Chicken Cutlets, a simple yet flavorful dish that highlights the ease and versatility of cooking with your Blackstone Griddle. Perfect for a quick and delicious dinner.

86. Grilled Lemon Pepper Tilapia

Portion Size: 2

Duration: 20 minutes

Ingredients:
- 2 tilapia fillets (about 6 ounces each)
- 2 teaspoons lemon pepper seasoning
- 1 tablespoon olive oil
- 1 lemon, sliced into rounds
- Salt, to taste
- Fresh parsley, chopped (for garnish)

Instructions:
1. **Preheat the Blackstone Griddle** over medium-high heat, aiming for a temperature of around 375°F (190°C).

2. **Season the Tilapia**: Sprinkle both sides of the tilapia fillets with lemon pepper seasoning and a pinch of salt.

3. **Oil the Griddle**: Lightly brush the griddle surface with olive oil to prevent the fish from sticking.

4. **Grill the Tilapia**: Place the tilapia fillets on the griddle. Cook for about 3-4 minutes on each side, or until the fish is opaque and flakes easily with a fork. Avoid flipping the fish too often to maintain its integrity.

5. **Add Lemon Slices**: In the last 2 minutes of cooking, place lemon slices around the tilapia on the griddle. Allow them to grill and caramelize, flipping once to enhance their flavor.

6. **Serve**: Transfer the grilled tilapia to plates. Garnish with grilled lemon slices and a sprinkle of fresh parsley.

Enjoy your Grilled Lemon Pepper Tilapia, a simple yet flavorful dish that showcases the ease and versatility of cooking with your Blackstone Griddle.

87. Griddled Asian Style Pork Chops

Portion Size: 2

Duration: 25 minutes

Ingredients:
- 2 pork chops, about 1 inch thick
- 2 tablespoons soy sauce
- 1 tablespoon honey
- 1 tablespoon olive oil, plus more for griddling
- 2 cloves garlic, minced

- 1 teaspoon ginger, grated
- 1/2 teaspoon ground black pepper
- 1/4 teaspoon red pepper flakes (optional for heat)
- 1 tablespoon green onions, finely sliced for garnish
- 1 teaspoon sesame seeds, for garnish

Instructions:

1. **Marinate the Pork Chops**: In a mixing bowl, combine soy sauce, honey, 1 tablespoon olive oil, minced garlic, grated ginger, black pepper, and red pepper flakes if using. Whisk together until well combined. Add the pork chops, ensuring they are fully coated in the marinade. Cover and let marinate in the refrigerator for at least 15 minutes, or up to 2 hours for deeper flavor.

2. **Preheat the Blackstone Griddle**: Turn your Blackstone griddle to medium-high heat and allow it to preheat for about 5 minutes. A properly preheated griddle ensures even cooking and perfect sear marks.

3. **Griddle the Pork Chops**: Remove the pork chops from the marinade, letting any excess drip off. Lightly oil the griddle surface with olive oil. Place the pork chops on the griddle and cook for about 5-7 minutes on each side, or until the internal temperature reaches 145°F (63°C) for medium-rare. Adjust the cooking time if you prefer your pork more or less done.

4. **Rest the Pork Chops**: Once cooked to your liking, transfer the pork chops to a plate and let them rest for 3-5 minutes. Resting allows the juices to redistribute throughout the meat, ensuring a moist and tender chop.

5. **Garnish and Serve**: Sprinkle the cooked pork chops with finely sliced green onions and sesame seeds for garnish. Serve immediately while hot.

Enjoy your Griddled Asian Style Pork Chops, a flavorful and easy-to-make dish that brings a touch of Asian cuisine to your Blackstone griddle cooking experience.

88. Grilled Caribbean Jerk Shrimp

Portion Size: 2

Duration: 25 minutes

Ingredients:
- 12 large shrimp, peeled and deveined
- 2 tablespoons Caribbean jerk seasoning
- 1 tablespoon olive oil
- 1 lime, juiced
- 2 cloves garlic, minced
- 1/2 red bell pepper, sliced into strips
- 1/2 yellow bell pepper, sliced into strips
- 1/2 onion, sliced
- 4 skewers (if using wooden skewers, soak in water for at least 30 minutes before grilling)
- Salt to taste
- Fresh cilantro for garnish

Instructions:

1. **Prep the Shrimp**: In a mixing bowl, combine shrimp, Caribbean jerk seasoning, olive oil, lime juice, and minced garlic. Toss until the shrimp are evenly coated. Let marinate for 15 minutes.

2. **Preheat the Griddle**: Turn your Blackstone griddle to medium-high heat, allowing it to warm up for about 5 minutes.

3. **Prepare the Vegetables**: While the griddle is heating, thread the sliced red and yellow bell peppers and onion slices onto the skewers, alternating between the vegetables. Sprinkle with a pinch of salt.

4. **Grill the Vegetables**: Place the vegetable skewers on the hot griddle. Grill for about 4-5 minutes on each side, or until they are tender and have charred edges. Remove from the griddle and set aside.

5. **Grill the Shrimp**: Thread the marinated shrimp onto the remaining skewers. Place the shrimp skewers on the griddle and cook for 2-3 minutes on each side, or until the shrimp are pink, firm, and cooked through.

6. **Serve**: Arrange the grilled shrimp and vegetable skewers on plates. Garnish with fresh cilantro. Serve immediately, offering a vibrant and flavorful Caribbean-inspired meal that's perfect for any dinner occasion on your Blackstone Griddle.

89. Griddled Maple Glazed Pork Belly

Portion Size: 2

Duration: 45 minutes

Ingredients:

- 1 lb pork belly, skin-on
- 2 tablespoons maple syrup
- 1 tablespoon soy sauce
- 1 tablespoon apple cider vinegar
- 1 teaspoon smoked paprika
- 1/2 teaspoon garlic powder
- 1/2 teaspoon onion powder
- Salt and pepper, to taste
- Olive oil, for griddling
- Green onions, sliced for garnish

Instructions:

1. **Prepare the Pork Belly**: Score the skin of the pork belly in a diamond pattern, being careful not to cut into the meat. This helps the fat render and the skin to crisp up.

2. **Marinate**: In a small bowl, mix together maple syrup, soy sauce, apple cider vinegar, smoked paprika, garlic powder, onion powder, salt, and pepper. Rub this mixture all over the pork belly, ensuring it gets into the scores. Let it marinate for at least 30 minutes, or overnight in the refrigerator for deeper flavor.

3. **Preheat the Griddle**: Turn your Blackstone griddle to medium heat and allow it to warm up. Brush the griddle surface with olive oil.

4. **Griddle the Pork Belly**: Place the pork belly skin-side down on the griddle. Cook for about 20 minutes, checking occasionally. The goal is to render the fat and crisp up the skin without burning.

5. **Flip and Glaze**: Carefully flip the pork belly to the meat side and brush with additional maple syrup. Cook for another 15-20 minutes, or until the internal temperature reaches 145°F (63°C). Baste with the glaze occasionally as it cooks.

6. **Rest and Slice**: Remove the pork belly from the griddle and let it rest for 10 minutes. This allows the juices to redistribute. Slice into thick pieces.

7. **Serve**: Arrange the sliced pork belly on a plate. Drizzle with any remaining glaze and garnish with sliced green onions. Serve immediately.

Enjoy your Griddled Maple Glazed Pork Belly, a sweet and savory delight that perfectly showcases the ease and versatility of cooking with your Blackstone Griddle.

90. Grilled Chipotle Lime Chicken

Portion Size: 2

Duration: 30 minutes

Ingredients:
- 2 chicken breasts, boneless and skinless
- 2 tablespoons olive oil
- 2 tablespoons chipotle peppers in adobo sauce, finely chopped
- Juice of 1 lime
- 1 teaspoon lime zest
- 1 garlic clove, minced
- 1/2 teaspoon ground cumin
- Salt and pepper, to taste
- Fresh cilantro, chopped (for garnish)
- Lime wedges, for serving

Instructions:

1. **Marinate the Chicken**: In a bowl, combine olive oil, chipotle peppers, lime juice, lime zest, minced garlic, ground cumin, salt, and pepper. Whisk until well mixed. Add the chicken breasts to the marinade, ensuring they are fully coated. Cover and refrigerate for at least 15 minutes, or up to 4 hours for deeper flavor.

2. **Preheat the Blackstone Griddle**: Turn your Blackstone Griddle to medium-high heat, allowing it to warm up for about 5 minutes.

3. **Grill the Chicken**: Remove the chicken from the marinade, letting the excess drip off. Place the chicken breasts on the hot griddle. Cook for about 6-7 minutes on each side, or until the internal temperature reaches 165°F (74°C) and the chicken is nicely charred on the outside.

4. **Rest the Chicken**: Once cooked, transfer the chicken to a cutting board and let it rest for a few minutes. This allows the juices to redistribute throughout the meat, ensuring it's moist and flavorful.

5. **Serve**: Slice the chicken into strips. Garnish with chopped fresh cilantro and serve with lime wedges on the side. Enjoy your Grilled Chipotle Lime Chicken as a flavorful and zesty main dish, perfect for a quick and satisfying dinner.

Chapter 5: 30 Sides and Snacks Recipes

91. Griddled Garlic Parmesan Asparagus

Portion Size: 2

Duration: 20 minutes

Ingredients:
- 1 bunch of asparagus, ends trimmed
- 2 tablespoons olive oil
- 3 cloves garlic, minced
- Salt and pepper, to taste
- 1/4 cup grated Parmesan cheese
- Lemon wedges, for serving

Instructions:
1. Preheat your Blackstone griddle over medium-high heat.

2. In a large bowl, toss the asparagus with olive oil, minced garlic, salt, and pepper until the asparagus is evenly coated.

3. Once the griddle is hot, lay the asparagus in a single layer across the surface. Avoid overcrowding to ensure each spear gets nicely charred.

4. Grill the asparagus for about 3-4 minutes on each side, or until they are tender and have grill marks.

5. Just before removing the asparagus from the griddle, sprinkle the grated Parmesan cheese evenly over the top. Allow the cheese to melt slightly, about 1 minute.

6. Transfer the asparagus to a serving platter. Serve immediately with lemon wedges on the side for a refreshing zest.

92. Grilled Corn on the Cob with Lime Butter

Portion Size: 2

Duration: 20 minutes

Ingredients:
- 4 ears of corn, husks and silk removed
- 4 tablespoons unsalted butter, at room temperature
- Zest of 1 lime
- 2 tablespoons lime juice
- 1 teaspoon chili powder
- Salt to taste
- Fresh cilantro, chopped (for garnish)

- Lime wedges, for serving

Instructions:

1. Preheat your Blackstone griddle to medium-high heat, around 375°F (190°C).

2. In a small bowl, mix together the softened butter, lime zest, lime juice, chili powder, and salt until well combined.

3. Place the ears of corn directly on the hot griddle. Cook for about 10-12 minutes, turning occasionally, until the corn is evenly charred on all sides.

4. Once the corn is grilled, remove from the griddle and immediately brush generously with the lime butter mixture, ensuring each ear is well coated.

5. Garnish the buttered corn with chopped cilantro.

6. Serve the grilled corn on the cob with additional lime wedges on the side.

Enjoy your Grilled Corn on the Cob with Lime Butter, a vibrant and flavorful side dish that perfectly complements any outdoor meal prepared on your Blackstone Griddle.

93. Griddle-Cooked Zucchini Fritters

Portion Size: 2

Duration: 30 minutes

Ingredients:
- 2 medium zucchinis, grated
- 1/4 cup all-purpose flour
- 1/4 cup grated Parmesan cheese
- 2 green onions, thinly sliced
- 1 large egg, beaten
- Salt and pepper, to taste
- 2 tablespoons olive oil, for griddling
- Sour cream or Greek yogurt, for serving (optional)

Instructions:

1. **Prepare the Zucchini**: Place the grated zucchini in a colander and sprinkle lightly with salt. Let it sit for 10 minutes, then squeeze out as much moisture as possible using a clean kitchen towel or paper towels.

2. **Mix the Fritter Batter**: In a large bowl, combine the drained zucchini, all-purpose flour, grated Parmesan cheese, thinly sliced green onions, and the beaten egg. Season with salt and pepper to taste. Stir until the mixture is well combined and holds together.

3. **Preheat the Griddle**: Heat your Blackstone griddle over medium heat. Drizzle the olive oil over the griddle surface to evenly coat.

4. **Form and Cook the Fritters**: Using your hands or a large spoon, form the zucchini mixture into small patties. Place the patties on the hot griddle, pressing them down slightly to flatten. Cook for about 4-5 minutes on each side, or until golden brown and crispy.

5. **Serve Hot**: Transfer the cooked zucchini fritters to a serving plate. Serve immediately while hot, accompanied by sour cream or Greek yogurt on the side if desired.

Enjoy your Griddle-Cooked Zucchini Fritters, a delicious and easy-to-make side dish that brings out the best flavors of zucchini, enhanced by the simplicity of cooking on your Blackstone Griddle.

94. Grilled Halloumi with Cherry Tomatoes

Portion Size: 2

Duration: 15 minutes

Ingredients:
- 8 oz halloumi cheese, sliced into 1/2-inch thick pieces
- 1 cup cherry tomatoes, halved
- 2 tablespoons olive oil
- 1/4 teaspoon salt
- 1/4 teaspoon black pepper
- 1 tablespoon balsamic glaze
- Fresh basil leaves, for garnish

Instructions:
1. Preheat your Blackstone griddle to medium-high heat, around 375°F (190°C).

2. Brush both sides of the halloumi slices with 1 tablespoon of olive oil. Season the cherry tomatoes with the remaining olive oil, salt, and pepper in a bowl.

3. Place the halloumi slices on the griddle. Grill for about 2-3 minutes on each side, or until golden brown and grill marks appear.

4. In the last minute of grilling the halloumi, add the seasoned cherry tomatoes to the griddle. Cook, stirring occasionally, until they are slightly charred and softened, about 1-2 minutes.

5. Remove the halloumi and cherry tomatoes from the griddle. Arrange the halloumi slices on a plate, top with the grilled cherry tomatoes, and drizzle with balsamic glaze.

6. Garnish with fresh basil leaves before serving. Enjoy your Grilled Halloumi with Cherry Tomatoes as a flavorful and easy-to-prepare side dish or snack, perfect for any grilling occasion.

95. Griddled Sweet Potato Wedges

Portion Size: 2

Duration: 25 minutes

Ingredients:
- 2 large sweet potatoes, peeled and cut into wedges
- 2 tablespoons olive oil
- 1 teaspoon smoked paprika
- 1/2 teaspoon garlic powder
- 1/2 teaspoon onion powder
- Salt and pepper, to taste
- Fresh parsley, chopped (for garnish)

- Optional: Ranch dressing or your favorite dipping sauce, for serving

Instructions:
1. Preheat your Blackstone griddle to medium-high heat, around 375°F (190°C).

2. In a large bowl, toss the sweet potato wedges with olive oil, smoked paprika, garlic powder, onion powder, salt, and pepper until they are evenly coated.

3. Arrange the seasoned sweet potato wedges in a single layer on the hot griddle. Cook for about 10-12 minutes, turning occasionally, until they are golden brown and tender.

4. Once cooked, transfer the sweet potato wedges to a serving platter. Garnish with chopped fresh parsley.

5. Serve immediately, accompanied by ranch dressing or your favorite dipping sauce if desired.

96. Grilled Jalapeño Poppers with Cream Cheese

Portion Size: 2

Duration: 20 minutes

Ingredients:
- 6 large jalapeños, halved and seeded
- 1 package (8 oz) cream cheese, softened
- 1/2 cup shredded sharp cheddar cheese
- 1/4 teaspoon garlic powder
- 1/4 teaspoon onion powder
- 1/4 teaspoon smoked paprika
- Salt and pepper to taste
- 12 slices of thin bacon
- Optional: chopped cilantro or green onions for garnish

Instructions:
1. **Prep the Jalapeños**: Halve the jalapeños lengthwise and remove the seeds and membranes. Set aside.

2. **Mix the Filling**: In a bowl, combine the softened cream cheese, shredded cheddar cheese, garlic powder, onion powder, smoked paprika, salt, and pepper. Mix until well combined.

3. **Fill the Jalapeños**: Spoon the cream cheese mixture into each jalapeño half, filling them generously.

4. **Wrap with Bacon**: Wrap each filled jalapeño half with a slice of bacon, securing the bacon with a toothpick if necessary. The bacon will help keep the filling in place while cooking.

5. **Preheat the Blackstone Griddle**: Turn your Blackstone Griddle to medium heat, allowing it to warm up for about 5 minutes.

6. **Grill the Poppers**: Place the bacon-wrapped jalapeños on the griddle, cheese side up. Grill for about 10 minutes, then carefully flip each popper using tongs. Continue grilling for another 8-10 minutes or until the bacon is crispy and the jalapeños are tender.

7. **Garnish and Serve**: Once cooked, transfer the jalapeño poppers to a serving plate. If desired, garnish with chopped cilantro or green onions. Serve warm as a delicious and spicy appetizer or side dish.

Enjoy your Grilled Jalapeño Poppers with Cream Cheese, a perfect blend of spicy, creamy, and crispy textures that make a great addition to any outdoor grilling session on your Blackstone Griddle.

97. *Griddle-Seared Brussels Sprouts with Bacon*

Portion Size: 2

Duration: 20 minutes

Ingredients:
- 1 lb Brussels sprouts, trimmed and halved
- 4 slices thick-cut bacon, cut into pieces
- 1 tablespoon olive oil
- Salt and pepper, to taste
- 2 tablespoons balsamic vinegar
- 1 teaspoon honey (optional)

Instructions:

1. Preheat your Blackstone griddle to medium-high heat, aiming for a surface temperature of around 375°F (190°C).

2. Spread the bacon pieces across the griddle. Cook, stirring occasionally, until the bacon is crispy and the fat has rendered, about 5-7 minutes. Use a slotted spatula to transfer the bacon to a paper towel-lined plate, leaving the bacon fat on the griddle.

3. In the bacon fat, add the Brussels sprouts, cut side down, to the griddle. Drizzle with olive oil and season with salt and pepper. Cook without moving them for about 5 minutes, or until the cut sides begin to char.

4. Stir the Brussels sprouts and continue cooking for another 5-10 minutes, until they are tender and caramelized on the edges. Adjust the heat if necessary to prevent burning.

5. In the last minute of cooking, add the cooked bacon back to the griddle with the Brussels sprouts. Drizzle balsamic vinegar and honey over the top, if using. Toss everything together and cook for another minute to glaze the Brussels sprouts and bacon.

6. Remove from the griddle and serve immediately. Enjoy your Griddle-Seared Brussels Sprouts with Bacon as a flavorful and hearty side dish perfect for any meal.

98. *Grilled Artichoke Hearts with Lemon Aioli*

Portion Size: 2

Duration: 20 minutes

Ingredients:
- 4 large artichoke hearts, halved
- 2 tablespoons olive oil
- Salt and pepper, to taste
- **For Lemon Aioli**:
  - 1/2 cup mayonnaise
  - 1 tablespoon lemon juice

- 1 teaspoon lemon zest
- 1 clove garlic, minced
- Salt and pepper, to taste

Instructions:

1. **Preheat the Blackstone Griddle** to medium-high heat, around 375°F (190°C).

2. **Prepare Artichokes**: Brush the artichoke hearts with olive oil and season with salt and pepper.

3. **Grill Artichokes**: Place the artichoke hearts cut side down on the griddle. Grill for about 5-7 minutes or until they are charred and tender. Flip and cook for an additional 3-5 minutes. Remove from the griddle and set aside.

4. **Make Lemon Aioli**: In a small bowl, combine mayonnaise, lemon juice, lemon zest, and minced garlic. Season with salt and pepper to taste. Whisk until smooth and well combined.

5. **Serve**: Arrange the grilled artichoke hearts on a plate and serve with the lemon aioli for dipping.

99. Griddled Cheesy Cauliflower Bites

Portion Size: 2

Duration: 30 minutes

Ingredients:
- 1 large head of cauliflower, cut into bite-sized florets
- 1/2 cup all-purpose flour
- 2 large eggs, beaten
- 1 cup panko breadcrumbs
- 1/2 cup grated Parmesan cheese
- 1 teaspoon garlic powder
- 1 teaspoon paprika
- Salt and pepper, to taste
- 1 cup shredded cheddar cheese
- Olive oil, for griddling
- Ranch dressing or your favorite dipping sauce, for serving

Instructions:

1. **Prep the Cauliflower**: Wash the cauliflower florets and pat them dry with paper towels. Ensure they are completely dry to help the coating stick.

2. **Set Up Dredging Station**: Arrange three shallow plates or bowls. In the first, place the all-purpose flour seasoned with salt and pepper. In the second, beat the eggs. In the third, mix together the panko breadcrumbs, grated Parmesan cheese, garlic powder, paprika, salt, and pepper.

3. **Dredge the Cauliflower**: Coat each cauliflower floret in the flour, shaking off the excess. Dip it into the beaten eggs, then dredge in the panko mixture, pressing to adhere the breadcrumbs.

4. **Preheat the Griddle**: Turn your Blackstone Griddle to medium heat and lightly oil the surface with olive oil.

5. **Griddle the Cauliflower**: Place the coated cauliflower bites on the griddle. Cook for about 3-4 minutes on each side or until golden brown and crispy. You may need to work in batches depending on the size of your griddle.

6. **Add Cheese**: Once all the cauliflower is cooked and still on the griddle, sprinkle the shredded cheddar cheese over the bites. Allow the cheese to melt for about 1-2 minutes.

7. **Serve**: Carefully remove the cheesy cauliflower bites from the griddle and serve immediately with ranch dressing or your favorite dipping sauce on the side.

Enjoy your Griddled Cheesy Cauliflower Bites, a delicious and easy-to-make side or snack that's perfect for any outdoor cooking occasion.

100. Grilled Stuffed Mini Bell Peppers

Portion Size: 2

Duration: 20 minutes

Ingredients:
- 10 mini bell peppers, halved and seeds removed
- 1/2 cup cream cheese, softened
- 1/4 cup shredded cheddar cheese
- 1/4 cup cooked and crumbled bacon
- 1 tablespoon green onions, finely chopped
- Salt and pepper, to taste
- Olive oil, for brushing

Instructions:

1. Preheat your Blackstone griddle to medium heat, approximately 350°F.

2. In a mixing bowl, combine cream cheese, shredded cheddar cheese, crumbled bacon, and green onions. Season with salt and pepper to taste. Mix until well combined.

3. Fill each mini bell pepper half with the cheese mixture, pressing gently to ensure the filling is secure.

4. Lightly brush the griddle with olive oil to prevent sticking. Place the stuffed bell peppers on the griddle, filling side up. Cook for about 10-12 minutes, or until the peppers are tender and the filling is warm and slightly golden on top.

5. Carefully remove the grilled stuffed mini bell peppers from the griddle using a spatula.

6. Serve immediately while warm, enjoying the creamy and savory flavors complemented by the slight char and sweetness of the grilled peppers.

101. Griddle-Cooked Spinach and Cheese Stuffed Mushrooms

Portion Size: 2

Duration: 30 minutes

Ingredients:
- 8 large mushrooms, stems removed
- 1 cup spinach, finely chopped

- 1/2 cup cream cheese, softened
- 1/4 cup grated Parmesan cheese
- 2 cloves garlic, minced
- 1 tablespoon olive oil
- Salt and pepper, to taste
- 1/4 cup shredded mozzarella cheese, for topping
- Fresh parsley, chopped, for garnish

Instructions:

1. **Preheat the Blackstone Griddle** over medium heat, aiming for a temperature of around 350°F (175°C).

2. **Prepare the Filling**: In a mixing bowl, combine the spinach, cream cheese, Parmesan cheese, minced garlic, salt, and pepper. Mix until well combined and creamy.

3. **Stuff the Mushrooms**: Using a small spoon, fill each mushroom cap generously with the spinach and cheese mixture. Press the mixture down slightly to pack it in.

4. **Griddle the Mushrooms**: Brush the griddle with olive oil to prevent sticking. Place the stuffed mushrooms on the griddle, filling side up. Cook for about 15-20 minutes, or until the mushrooms are tender and the filling is heated through.

5. **Add Mozzarella Cheese**: A few minutes before the mushrooms are done, sprinkle the shredded mozzarella cheese over the top of each mushroom. Continue cooking until the cheese is melted and bubbly.

6. **Garnish and Serve**: Once cooked, carefully remove the mushrooms from the griddle using a spatula. Garnish with chopped fresh parsley. Serve hot as a delicious and easy side dish or appetizer.

Enjoy your Griddle-Cooked Spinach and Cheese Stuffed Mushrooms, a savory and satisfying treat that's perfect for any outdoor cooking occasion, showcasing the versatility and convenience of your Blackstone Griddle.

102. Grilled Avocado with Lime and Chili

Portion Size: 2

Duration: 15 minutes

Ingredients:
- 2 ripe avocados, halved and pitted
- 1 tablespoon olive oil
- Salt and pepper, to taste
- 1 lime, cut into wedges
- 1 teaspoon chili flakes (adjust to taste)
- Fresh cilantro, for garnish (optional)

Instructions:

1. Preheat your Blackstone griddle over medium heat.

2. Brush the cut sides of the avocados with olive oil and season with salt and pepper.

3. Place the avocados cut side down on the griddle. Cook for about 5-7 minutes, or until they have nice grill marks and are slightly softened.

4. Carefully remove the avocados from the griddle using a spatula. Squeeze lime wedges over the grilled avocados according to taste.

5. Sprinkle the chili flakes evenly over the avocados. Adjust the amount based on your preference for heat.

6. Garnish with fresh cilantro if desired.

7. Serve immediately as a flavorful and unique side dish or snack, perfect for any grilling occasion.

103. Griddled Rosemary Garlic Flatbread

Portion Size: 2

Duration: 20 minutes

Ingredients:
- 1 cup all-purpose flour
- 2 teaspoons baking powder
- 1/2 teaspoon salt
- 1 tablespoon fresh rosemary, finely chopped
- 2 cloves garlic, minced
- 3/4 cup water
- 2 tablespoons olive oil, plus more for brushing

Instructions:

1. In a large mixing bowl, whisk together the all-purpose flour, baking powder, and salt.

2. Stir in the finely chopped fresh rosemary and minced garlic until evenly distributed throughout the flour mixture.

3. Gradually add water to the dry ingredients, stirring continuously until a soft dough forms. If the dough feels too sticky, add a little more flour, one tablespoon at a time, until it reaches a manageable consistency.

4. Divide the dough into two equal portions. On a lightly floured surface, roll out each portion into a thin circle, about 1/4 inch thick.

5. Preheat your Blackstone griddle over medium-high heat. Lightly brush the griddle surface with olive oil.

6. Carefully transfer one flatbread onto the hot griddle. Cook for about 2-3 minutes on one side, or until bubbles form on the surface and the bottom is golden brown with charred spots.

7. Brush the top of the flatbread with a little olive oil, then flip it using a spatula. Cook for an additional 2-3 minutes on the other side until it is also golden brown and crispy.

8. Remove the cooked flatbread from the griddle and place it on a serving plate. Repeat the process with the second portion of dough.

9. Serve the griddled rosemary garlic flatbread warm, as a side dish or with your favorite dips and toppings.

104. Grilled Buffalo Cauliflower Bites

Portion Size: 2

⏳ Duration: 30 minutes

🛒 Ingredients:
- 1 large head of cauliflower, cut into bite-sized florets
- 1/2 cup all-purpose flour
- 1/2 cup water
- 1 teaspoon garlic powder
- 1/2 teaspoon salt
- 1/4 teaspoon black pepper
- 1/2 cup buffalo sauce
- 1 tablespoon unsalted butter, melted
- Ranch or blue cheese dressing, for serving
- Celery sticks, for serving

👨‍🍳 Instructions:

1. In a large bowl, whisk together the flour, water, garlic powder, salt, and black pepper until smooth. Add the cauliflower florets to the bowl and toss until they are fully coated with the batter.

2. Preheat your Blackstone griddle over medium-high heat. Lightly oil the griddle surface to prevent sticking.

3. Carefully place the battered cauliflower florets on the griddle. Cook for about 5-7 minutes on each side, or until they are golden brown and crispy. You may need to work in batches depending on the size of your griddle.

4. While the cauliflower is cooking, combine the buffalo sauce and melted butter in a small bowl. Mix well to create the buffalo coating.

5. Once the cauliflower is cooked, transfer the florets to a large bowl. Pour the buffalo sauce mixture over the cooked cauliflower and toss to coat evenly.

6. Serve the buffalo cauliflower bites immediately with ranch or blue cheese dressing and celery sticks on the side. Enjoy a spicy, flavorful snack that's perfect for any grilling occasion.

105. Griddle-Seared Polenta Cakes with Marinara

🍽 Portion Size: 2

⏳ Duration: 30 minutes

🛒 Ingredients:
- 1 cup polenta
- 4 cups water
- 1 teaspoon salt
- 2 tablespoons unsalted butter
- 1/2 cup grated Parmesan cheese
- 1 cup marinara sauce
- Olive oil, for griddling
- Fresh basil leaves, for garnish

👨‍🍳 Instructions:

1. **Cook Polenta**: In a medium saucepan, bring water and salt to a boil. Gradually whisk in polenta. Reduce heat to low and cook, stirring frequently, until polenta thickens and water is fully absorbed, about 15-20 minutes. Remove from heat and stir in butter and Parmesan cheese until well combined.

2. **Cool and Shape**: Pour the cooked polenta onto a greased baking sheet, spreading it out to about 1/2-inch thickness. Allow to cool at room temperature, then refrigerate for at least 1 hour, or until firm.

3. **Cut Polenta**: Once firm, use a cookie cutter or knife to cut the polenta into circles or squares, depending on your preference.

4. **Preheat the Blackstone Griddle**: Turn your Blackstone griddle to medium-high heat, allowing it to warm up for about 5 minutes.

5. **Griddle Polenta Cakes**: Brush both sides of each polenta cake with olive oil. Place them on the hot griddle and cook for about 3-4 minutes on each side, or until they are golden brown and crispy on the outside.

6. **Warm Marinara Sauce**: While polenta cakes are griddling, warm the marinara sauce in a saucepan over low heat or directly on the griddle if space allows.

7. **Serve**: Arrange the griddled polenta cakes on plates. Spoon warm marinara sauce over the cakes. Garnish with fresh basil leaves.

Enjoy your Griddle-Seared Polenta Cakes with Marinara, a simple yet elegant dish that brings the comforting flavors of Italian cuisine to your outdoor griddle cooking.

106. Grilled Peach and Burrata Salad

Portion Size: 2

Duration: 20 minutes

Ingredients:
- 2 ripe peaches, halved and pitted
- 1 tablespoon olive oil
- 4 ounces burrata cheese
- 1/4 cup balsamic glaze
- 1/2 cup arugula
- Salt and pepper, to taste
- Fresh basil leaves, for garnish

Instructions:
1. Preheat your Blackstone griddle to medium-high heat, around 375°F (190°C).

2. Brush the peach halves with olive oil on all sides. Season lightly with salt and pepper.

3. Place the peach halves cut side down onto the hot griddle. Grill for about 4-5 minutes, or until the peaches have nice grill marks and start to soften. Flip and grill for another 2-3 minutes on the skin side. Remove from the griddle and let cool slightly.

4. On a serving plate, arrange the arugula as a bed for the peaches and burrata.

5. Place the grilled peach halves on top of the arugula. Tear the burrata cheese open and place it in the center of the plate, allowing it to spread out among the peaches.

6. Drizzle the balsamic glaze over the peaches and burrata.

7. Garnish with fresh basil leaves. Season with a pinch of salt and pepper to taste.

8. Serve immediately, enjoying the blend of warm grilled peaches with the cool, creamy burrata and the tangy balsamic glaze.

107. Griddled Eggplant Caponata

Portion Size: 2

Duration: 30 minutes

Ingredients:
- 1 large eggplant, cut into 1/2-inch cubes
- 2 tablespoons olive oil
- Salt and pepper, to taste
- 1 small onion, diced
- 2 cloves garlic, minced
- 1 bell pepper, diced
- 1/4 cup capers, rinsed
- 1/4 cup pitted green olives, chopped
- 1 can (14 oz) diced tomatoes, drained
- 2 tablespoons balsamic vinegar
- 1 teaspoon sugar
- 1/4 cup fresh basil, chopped

Instructions:
1. Preheat your Blackstone griddle to medium-high heat.

2. In a large bowl, toss the eggplant cubes with 1 tablespoon of olive oil, salt, and pepper until evenly coated.

3. Spread the eggplant cubes on the griddle and cook for about 10-12 minutes, stirring occasionally, until they are golden brown and softened. Transfer the cooked eggplant to a bowl and set aside.

4. Reduce the griddle heat to medium. Add the remaining tablespoon of olive oil to the griddle. Add the diced onion and minced garlic, cooking for about 3-4 minutes until the onion is translucent.

5. Stir in the diced bell pepper, capers, and chopped olives. Cook for another 5 minutes, until the bell pepper is softened.

6. Return the cooked eggplant to the griddle. Add the drained diced tomatoes, balsamic vinegar, and sugar. Stir well to combine all the ingredients. Cook for an additional 5-7 minutes, allowing the flavors to meld together and the mixture to thicken slightly.

7. Remove the griddle from the heat. Stir in the chopped fresh basil and adjust the seasoning with additional salt and pepper if needed.

8. Serve the eggplant caponata warm or at room temperature, as a delightful side dish or a topping for grilled bread.

108. Grilled Pineapple Salsa

🍽 Portion Size: 2
⏳ Duration: 20 minutes
🛒 Ingredients:
- 1/2 fresh pineapple, peeled, cored, and cut into 1/2-inch thick rings
- 1 small red onion, finely chopped
- 1 jalapeño, seeded and finely diced
- 1/4 cup fresh cilantro, chopped
- Juice of 1 lime
- Salt to taste

✳ Instructions:
1. Preheat your Blackstone griddle to medium-high heat, around 375°F (190°C).

2. Place the pineapple rings directly on the griddle. Grill for about 2-3 minutes on each side, or until they have nice grill marks and are slightly caramelized. Remove from the griddle and let cool for a few minutes.

3. Once cooled, dice the grilled pineapple into small pieces and transfer to a mixing bowl.

4. Add the chopped red onion, diced jalapeño, and chopped cilantro to the bowl with the pineapple.

5. Squeeze the juice of one lime over the mixture and add salt to taste. Stir well to combine all the ingredients.

6. Serve the Grilled Pineapple Salsa with your favorite grilled dishes or enjoy it with tortilla chips as a refreshing appetizer.

109. Griddle-Cooked Cheese-Stuffed Jalapeños

🍽 Portion Size: 2
⏳ Duration: 20 minutes
🛒 Ingredients:
- 6 large jalapeños
- 1 cup cream cheese, softened
- 1/2 cup shredded sharp cheddar cheese
- 1/4 teaspoon garlic powder
- 1/4 teaspoon onion powder
- Salt and pepper to taste
- 12 slices of thin bacon
- Toothpicks

✳ Instructions:
1. Preheat your Blackstone griddle to medium heat, around 350°F.

2. Slice each jalapeño in half lengthwise. Using a spoon, scrape out the seeds and membranes to create a hollow for the filling.

3. In a mixing bowl, combine cream cheese, shredded cheddar cheese, garlic powder, onion powder, salt, and pepper. Mix until well combined.

4. Fill each jalapeño half with the cheese mixture, spreading it evenly.

5. Wrap each stuffed jalapeño half with a slice of bacon, securing the bacon with a toothpick. Ensure the bacon is snug but not too tight.

6. Lightly oil the griddle surface with a brush or spray to prevent sticking.

7. Place the bacon-wrapped jalapeños on the griddle, cheese side up, and cook for about 5-7 minutes. Carefully flip each jalapeño and cook for an additional 5-7 minutes, or until the bacon is crispy and the peppers are tender.

8. Transfer the cooked jalapeños to a plate lined with paper towels to absorb any excess grease.

9. Serve warm as a delicious and spicy appetizer or side dish, perfect for any grilling occasion.

110. Grilled Garlic Herb Potato Skewers

Portion Size: 2

Duration: 30 minutes

Ingredients:
- 1 lb baby potatoes, halved
- 2 tablespoons olive oil
- 1 teaspoon garlic powder
- 1 teaspoon dried rosemary
- 1 teaspoon dried thyme
- Salt and pepper, to taste
- Wooden skewers (soaked in water for at least 30 minutes to prevent burning)

Instructions:

1. Preheat your Blackstone griddle to medium-high heat, around 375°F (190°C).

2. In a large bowl, toss the halved baby potatoes with olive oil, garlic powder, dried rosemary, dried thyme, salt, and pepper until well coated.

3. Thread the seasoned potatoes onto the soaked wooden skewers, leaving a small space between each potato to ensure even cooking.

4. Place the potato skewers on the hot griddle. Cook for about 15-20 minutes, turning every 5 minutes, until the potatoes are golden brown on the outside and tender on the inside.

5. Check the doneness of the potatoes by piercing them with a fork. If the fork slides in easily, the potatoes are cooked.

6. Remove the potato skewers from the griddle and let them cool for a minute before serving.

Enjoy your Grilled Garlic Herb Potato Skewers, a simple yet delicious side dish that complements any meal cooked on your Blackstone Griddle.

111. Griddled Crispy Chickpeas with Smoked Paprika

Portion Size: 2

Duration: 20 minutes

Ingredients:

- 1 can (15 oz) chickpeas, drained and patted dry
- 2 tablespoons olive oil
- 1 teaspoon smoked paprika
- 1/2 teaspoon garlic powder
- Salt to taste
- Freshly ground black pepper to taste
- Optional: 1/4 teaspoon cayenne pepper for extra heat

Instructions:

1. Preheat your Blackstone griddle over medium-high heat, aiming for a surface temperature of around 375°F (190°C).

2. In a mixing bowl, toss the dried chickpeas with olive oil, smoked paprika, garlic powder, salt, black pepper, and cayenne pepper (if using) until evenly coated.

3. Spread the seasoned chickpeas in a single layer on the hot griddle. Cook for about 10-12 minutes, stirring occasionally, until they are golden brown and crispy.

4. Once the chickpeas have achieved a crispy texture, use a metal spatula to transfer them to a serving bowl or plate.

5. Serve the griddled crispy chickpeas immediately as a savory, crunchy snack or side dish. They can also be allowed to cool and stored in an airtight container for a grab-and-go snack.

112. Grilled Lemon Basil Shrimp Skewers

Portion Size: 2

Duration: 20 minutes

Ingredients:
- 12 large shrimp, peeled and deveined
- 2 tablespoons olive oil
- 1 tablespoon fresh lemon juice
- 1 tablespoon fresh basil, finely chopped
- Salt and pepper, to taste
- 4 wooden skewers, soaked in water for at least 30 minutes

Instructions:

1. **Preheat the Blackstone Griddle** to medium-high heat, aiming for a surface temperature of around 375°F (190°C).

2. **Prepare the Shrimp**: In a mixing bowl, combine the shrimp, olive oil, lemon juice, chopped basil, salt, and pepper. Toss until the shrimp are evenly coated with the marinade.

3. **Skewer the Shrimp**: Thread 3 shrimp onto each soaked wooden skewer, leaving a small space between each shrimp to ensure even cooking.

4. **Grill the Skewers**: Place the shrimp skewers on the hot griddle. Grill for about 2-3 minutes on each side, or until the shrimp are pink and opaque.

5. **Serve**: Remove the shrimp skewers from the griddle and serve immediately. Enjoy your Grilled Lemon Basil Shrimp Skewers as a flavorful and easy-to-prepare side or snack, perfect for any outdoor grilling occasion.

113. Griddle-Seared Sweet Corn Fritters

Portion Size: 2

Duration: 30 minutes

Ingredients:
- 1 cup fresh sweet corn kernels (about 2 ears of corn)
- 1/4 cup all-purpose flour
- 1/4 cup cornmeal
- 1/4 cup shredded cheddar cheese
- 1/4 cup milk
- 1 large egg
- 2 green onions, finely chopped
- 1 small jalapeño, seeded and minced (optional for heat)
- Salt and pepper, to taste
- 2 tablespoons vegetable oil, for griddling

Instructions:

1. **Combine Dry Ingredients**: In a large bowl, mix together the flour, cornmeal, shredded cheddar cheese, a pinch of salt, and pepper until well combined.

2. **Add Corn and Wet Ingredients**: Stir in the sweet corn kernels, chopped green onions, and minced jalapeño (if using) to the dry mixture. Add the milk and egg, stirring until the batter is just combined. Be careful not to overmix.

3. **Preheat the Griddle**: Heat your Blackstone Griddle over medium heat. Once hot, brush the griddle surface with vegetable oil to prevent sticking.

4. **Cook the Fritters**: Scoop 1/4 cup portions of the batter onto the griddle, flattening them slightly with the back of the scoop to form fritters. Cook for about 4-5 minutes on each side, or until they are golden brown and crispy.

5. **Serve Hot**: Remove the fritters from the griddle and place them on a paper towel-lined plate to drain any excess oil. Serve the sweet corn fritters hot, accompanied by your favorite dipping sauce or as a side to your main dish.

Enjoy your Griddle-Seared Sweet Corn Fritters, a delightful and easy-to-make side that perfectly complements any meal, bringing out the natural sweetness of corn with a crispy exterior.

114. Grilled Balsamic Glazed Portobello Mushrooms

Portion Size: 2

Duration: 20 minutes

Ingredients:
- 4 large Portobello mushrooms, stems removed
- 1/4 cup balsamic vinegar
- 2 tablespoons olive oil
- 2 cloves garlic, minced

- Salt and pepper, to taste
- 1 teaspoon dried thyme
- 1 teaspoon dried rosemary

Instructions:

1. In a small bowl, whisk together balsamic vinegar, olive oil, minced garlic, salt, pepper, dried thyme, and dried rosemary to create the marinade.

2. Place the Portobello mushrooms in a large dish or resealable plastic bag. Pour the marinade over the mushrooms, ensuring they are well coated on both sides. Let them marinate for at least 10 minutes, or up to 30 minutes for deeper flavor.

3. Preheat your Blackstone griddle to medium-high heat, around 375°F (190°C).

4. Once the griddle is hot, place the marinated Portobello mushrooms on the surface, reserving any leftover marinade for basting. Grill for about 4-5 minutes on each side, basting with the remaining marinade occasionally, until the mushrooms are tender and have grill marks.

5. Serve the grilled Portobello mushrooms hot, garnished with additional fresh herbs if desired.

115. Griddled BBQ Cauliflower Bites

Portion Size: 2

Duration: 25 minutes

Ingredients:
- 1 large head of cauliflower, cut into bite-sized florets
- 2 tablespoons olive oil
- 1/2 cup BBQ sauce
- Salt and pepper, to taste
- Optional garnishes: chopped green onions, sesame seeds

Instructions:

1. Preheat your Blackstone griddle over medium-high heat.

2. In a large bowl, toss the cauliflower florets with olive oil, salt, and pepper until they are evenly coated.

3. Arrange the cauliflower florets in a single layer on the griddle. Cook for about 10-12 minutes, turning occasionally, until they are golden brown and slightly charred on the edges.

4. Brush the BBQ sauce over the cauliflower florets, turning them to ensure they are well coated on all sides. Cook for an additional 3-5 minutes, allowing the BBQ sauce to caramelize slightly.

5. Remove the cauliflower from the griddle and transfer to a serving dish. If desired, sprinkle with optional garnishes like chopped green onions and sesame seeds.

Enjoy your Griddled BBQ Cauliflower Bites, a delicious and easy side dish that brings a smoky sweetness to your outdoor grilling experience.

116. Grilled Watermelon and Feta Salad

🍽 Portion Size: 2

⏳ Duration: 15 minutes

🛒 Ingredients:
- 4 thick slices of watermelon, about 1 inch thick
- 1/2 cup feta cheese, crumbled
- 2 tablespoons balsamic glaze
- 1/4 cup fresh mint leaves, roughly chopped
- 2 tablespoons olive oil
- Salt and pepper, to taste
- Optional: arugula or mixed greens for serving

Instructions:

1. Preheat your Blackstone griddle to medium-high heat, aiming for a temperature around 400°F.

2. Brush each watermelon slice lightly with olive oil on both sides. Season with a pinch of salt.

3. Place the watermelon slices on the griddle. Grill for about 2-3 minutes on each side, or until grill marks appear and the watermelon is slightly softened.

4. Remove the grilled watermelon slices from the griddle and let them cool for a minute. Cut into bite-sized cubes if desired.

5. Arrange the watermelon on plates over a bed of arugula or mixed greens if using.

6. Sprinkle the crumbled feta cheese and chopped mint leaves over the grilled watermelon.

7. Drizzle balsamic glaze over the top of each salad. Season with freshly ground black pepper to taste.

8. Serve immediately, enjoying the refreshing combination of sweet grilled watermelon, tangy feta, and the rich balsamic glaze.

117. Griddle-Cooked Spinach Artichoke Dip

🍽 Portion Size: 2

⏳ Duration: 25 minutes

🛒 Ingredients:
- 1 cup artichoke hearts, drained and chopped
- 1 cup fresh spinach, roughly chopped
- 1/2 cup sour cream
- 1/4 cup mayonnaise
- 1/2 cup cream cheese, softened
- 1/2 cup Parmesan cheese, grated
- 1 clove garlic, minced
- Salt and pepper to taste
- 1 tablespoon olive oil
- 1/4 cup mozzarella cheese, shredded for topping

Instructions:

1. **Preheat the Blackstone Griddle** to medium heat, aiming for a surface temperature of around 350°F (175°C).

2. **Mix the Dip Ingredients**: In a large bowl, combine artichoke hearts, spinach, sour cream, mayonnaise, cream cheese, Parmesan cheese, minced garlic, salt, and pepper. Stir until all ingredients are well mixed and the mixture is smooth.

3. **Prepare the Griddle**: Lightly brush the griddle surface with olive oil to prevent sticking.

4. **Cook the Dip**: Transfer the dip mixture to a cast iron skillet or a heavy-duty aluminum foil pan that is safe for griddle use. Place the skillet or pan on the griddle.

5. **Melt and Mix**: Allow the dip to heat through, stirring occasionally, for about 10-15 minutes. The dip should become warm and the cheeses well melted.

6. **Add the Topping**: Sprinkle the shredded mozzarella cheese over the top of the dip. Cover the skillet or pan with a lid or aluminum foil to help the mozzarella cheese melt, about 3-5 minutes.

7. **Serve Warm**: Once the cheese is melted and bubbly, carefully remove the skillet or pan from the griddle. Serve the spinach artichoke dip warm with your choice of tortilla chips, sliced baguette, or fresh vegetables for dipping.

Enjoy your Griddle-Cooked Spinach Artichoke Dip, a creamy and savory side perfect for any outdoor gathering or a cozy night in, easily prepared on your Blackstone Griddle.

118. Grilled Prosciutto-Wrapped Asparagus

Portion Size: 2

Duration: 15 minutes

Ingredients:
- 1 bunch of asparagus (about 20 spears), tough ends trimmed
- 10 slices of prosciutto, thinly sliced
- 1 tablespoon olive oil
- Salt and freshly ground black pepper, to taste
- Optional: Shaved Parmesan cheese for garnish

Instructions:
1. Preheat your Blackstone griddle to medium-high heat, around 375°F (190°C).

2. Lightly brush the asparagus spears with olive oil. Season with salt and pepper.

3. Take a slice of prosciutto and wrap it around the middle of an asparagus spear, leaving the tips exposed. Repeat with the remaining asparagus and prosciutto.

4. Place the prosciutto-wrapped asparagus on the hot griddle. Cook for about 2-3 minutes on each side, or until the prosciutto is crispy and the asparagus is tender and slightly charred.

5. Once cooked, transfer the asparagus to a serving plate. If desired, garnish with shaved Parmesan cheese.

6. Serve immediately while hot, enjoying the savory crunch of prosciutto with the tender, grilled asparagus.

119. Griddled Chimichurri Grilled Vegetables

- Portion Size: 2
- Duration: 20 minutes
- Ingredients:
- 1 zucchini, sliced into 1/4-inch rounds
- 1 yellow squash, sliced into 1/4-inch rounds
- 1 red bell pepper, cut into 1-inch pieces
- 1 yellow bell pepper, cut into 1-inch pieces
- 1 red onion, cut into wedges
- 2 tablespoons olive oil
- Salt and pepper, to taste
- **For the Chimichurri Sauce:**
  - 1/2 cup fresh parsley, finely chopped
  - 1/4 cup olive oil
  - 2 tablespoons red wine vinegar
  - 2 garlic cloves, minced
  - 1/2 teaspoon red pepper flakes
  - 1/2 teaspoon salt
  - 1/4 teaspoon black pepper

Instructions:

1. **Prepare the Chimichurri Sauce**: In a small bowl, combine the chopped parsley, olive oil, red wine vinegar, minced garlic, red pepper flakes, salt, and black pepper. Stir well until all ingredients are thoroughly mixed. Set aside to let the flavors meld.

2. **Preheat the Blackstone Griddle**: Turn your Blackstone Griddle to medium-high heat, allowing it to warm up for about 5 minutes.

3. **Season the Vegetables**: In a large bowl, toss the zucchini, yellow squash, red bell pepper, yellow bell pepper, and red onion with 2 tablespoons of olive oil. Season with salt and pepper to taste, ensuring all the vegetables are evenly coated.

4. **Griddle the Vegetables**: Spread the seasoned vegetables evenly across the hot griddle. Cook for about 10-12 minutes, turning occasionally, until the vegetables are tender and have charred edges.

5. **Serve with Chimichurri Sauce**: Once the vegetables are cooked, transfer them to a serving platter. Drizzle the chimichurri sauce over the grilled vegetables or serve it on the side for dipping.

Enjoy your Griddled Chimichurri Grilled Vegetables, a vibrant and flavorful side dish that brings a fresh twist to your outdoor grilling experience.

120. Grilled Tomato and Mozzarella Skewers

- Portion Size: 2
- Duration: 20 minutes

Ingredients:
- 1 large tomato, cut into 1/2-inch thick slices
- 8 ounces fresh mozzarella cheese, cut into 1/4-inch thick slices

- 1/4 cup fresh basil leaves
- 2 tablespoons balsamic glaze
- 2 tablespoons olive oil
- Salt and pepper, to taste
- Wooden skewers, soaked in water for at least 30 minutes

Instructions:

1. Preheat your Blackstone griddle to medium heat, around 350°F (175°C).

2. Assemble the skewers by alternating a slice of tomato, a basil leaf, and a slice of mozzarella cheese until the skewer is filled. Repeat the process for all skewers.

3. Lightly brush each side of the assembled skewers with olive oil and season with salt and pepper.

4. Place the skewers on the hot griddle and cook for 2-3 minutes on each side, or until the cheese starts to melt and the tomatoes are slightly charred.

5. Carefully remove the skewers from the griddle and drizzle with balsamic glaze.

6. Serve immediately, enjoying the warm, melted mozzarella paired with the fresh taste of tomato and basil, enhanced by the sweet and tangy balsamic glaze.

Conclusion

Throughout this guide, you have gathered a thorough set of techniques and insights crucial for mastering the art of Blackstone grilling. Each chapter has been carefully crafted to lead you from the initial setup of your griddle to the nuanced process of achieving a perfect steak sear. Exploring the intricacies of grilling on a Blackstone invites a continuous journey through diverse flavors, advanced techniques, and the pleasure of sharing these well-crafted culinary creations with friends and family.

Engage in thoughtful experimentation with your Blackstone Griddle, a versatile cooking surface that opens up a wide range of culinary possibilities. For example, think about creating a new spice blend by skillfully balancing cumin, smoked paprika, and garlic powder to elevate the flavor of your favorite cuts of meat, such as ribeye or pork tenderloin. Alternatively, dive into the world of griddle-baked desserts by carefully controlling the griddle's temperature to achieve perfect caramelization of sugars in dishes like apple cinnamon pancakes or chocolate chip cookie skillets. Each culinary adventure offers a unique chance to refine your grilling skills and treat your palate to delightful flavors.

Incorporating seasonal ingredients is essential for enhancing the flavor complexity of your dishes. Challenge yourself to seek out fresh, seasonal produce and ethically raised meats from local farmers' markets. For example, in spring, include tender asparagus and sweet strawberries in your recipes, while in fall, focus on hearty squashes and earthy mushrooms. This approach not only supports your local economy by backing regional farmers but also ensures that you're using ingredients at their peak freshness and flavor, which enhances the overall quality of your grilled creations.

Immerse yourself in the lively Blackstone grilling community to broaden your knowledge and sharpen your skills. Actively participate in specialized online forums, connect with dedicated social media groups, and attend local cooking classes designed for Blackstone enthusiasts. These platforms provide a wealth of information, from addressing common technical challenges like uneven heating or seasoning maintenance to discovering innovative recipes that redefine traditional grilling. By sharing your own experiences and culinary successes, you can inspire others and build meaningful connections with fellow grilling lovers who share your enthusiasm for this culinary art form.

Ensuring safety is crucial when operating your Blackstone Griddle, and it all starts with choosing the right spot for it. The griddle should be placed on a surface that is not just flat but also sturdy, preventing any chance of tipping or wobbling while in use. This is essential since any instability can lead to risky situations, particularly when handling high temperatures and open flames. The surface must be strong enough to support the griddle's weight, along with any extra cooking gear or ingredients, without shifting.

A thorough inspection of the gas connections and hoses is important to spot any potential leaks, which could create a serious safety risk. To carry out this inspection, prepare a solution made of water and mild detergent, ensuring it's well mixed for a soapy consistency. Generously apply this solution to all connections and hoses, covering every inch where a gas leak might occur. Keep a close eye on the area; the appearance of bubbles indicates a gas leak, which requires immediate attention and repair. This proactive step is vital for maintaining a safe cooking environment by avoiding the buildup of flammable gas.

Proper maintenance, storage, and winterization practices are essential for extending the life and performance of your Blackstone Griddle, especially in areas that experience harsh winter conditions. Start by thoroughly cleaning the griddle surface to eliminate any leftover food particles or grease, which can lead to corrosion or attract pests during storage. Once cleaned, apply a thin layer of oil to season the griddle, forming a protective barrier against rust. Disconnect the propane tank from the griddle; this crucial safety step prevents gas leaks during storage. Store the propane tank in a cool, dry location, ensuring it's out of direct sunlight and extreme temperature shifts. Use a weather-resistant cover to protect the griddle from the elements. If you're storing it outdoors, choose a spot that offers extra protection from moisture, like under a covered patio or in a garage, to reduce the risks posed by rain and freezing conditions.

Setting specific, achievable culinary milestones on your Blackstone Griddle can greatly enhance your cooking skills and expand your culinary horizons. Begin by mastering fundamental techniques, such as achieving the perfect sear on a smash burger, which requires precise temperature control and timing to develop a flavorful crust while keeping it juicy. Move on to more intricate tasks, like obtaining a balanced char on a mix of vegetables, which involves understanding the different cooking times and heat needs of various produce. Additionally, explore the griddle's versatility by trying international dishes, adapting classic recipes to fit the unique cooking surface. Each milestone you reach not only sharpens your abilities but also enriches your culinary repertoire, allowing you to confidently host gatherings where you can showcase your grilling skills through the preparation of delicious, freshly grilled dishes.

The essence of Blackstone grilling goes beyond just cooking; it's deeply connected to the shared experiences and interactions that happen around the griddle. The communal nature of grilling creates an atmosphere where laughter and conversation flow freely, making lasting memories. To keep this vibrant spirit alive, always look for new recipes and innovative techniques that challenge and inspire you. Embrace the wealth of culinary knowledge available through various media and communities, using it to ignite your passion for grilling. Your Blackstone Griddle acts as a gateway to a vast world of culinary discovery and social connection, providing endless opportunities to create cherished moments through the art of grilling.

www.ingramcontent.com/pod-product-compliance
Lightning Source LLC
Chambersburg PA
CBHW050749100426
42744CB00012BA/1949